20 EVENTS

Discoveries

THAT CHANGED SCIENCE

LOIS MARKHAM

RSVP

RAINTREE STECK-VAUGHN
P U B L I S H E R S

The Steck-Vaughn Company

Austin, Texas

Consultant: Julie Ealy, Science Department, The Peddie School, Hightstown, New Jersey

Developed for Steck-Vaughn Company by
Visual Education Corporation, Princeton, New Jersey

Project Director: Jewel Moulthrop
Editor: Michael Gee
Copy Editor: Margaret P. Roeske
Editorial Assistants: Carol Ciaston, Stacy Tibbetts
Photo Research: Martin A. Levick
Production Supervisor: Maureen Ryan Pancza
Proofreading Management: William A. Murray
Word Processing: Cynthia C. Feldner
Interior Design: Maxson Crandall, Lee Grabarczyk
Cover Design: Maxson Crandall
Page Layout: Maxson Crandall, Lisa Evans-Skopas, Christine Osborne

Raintree Steck-Vaughn Publishers staff

Editor: Shirley Shalit
Project Manager: Joyce Spicer

Printed and bound in the United States

1 2 3 4 5 6 7 8 9 0   VH   99 98 97 96 95 94

Cover: Experiments with electricity in the 1700s led to the invention of the incandescent light bulb (inset) in 1879 and to the eventual lighting of cities. The background photo shows Seattle, Washington.

Credits and Acknowledgments
Cover photos: Jim Corwin/Photo Researchers (background); U. S. Department of the Interior, National Park Service, Edison National Historic Site (inset)
Illustrations: Parrot Graphics, Precision Graphics

4: Erich Lessing/Art Resource; **5:** Mary Evans Picture Library/Photo Researchers; **6:** National Library of Medicine; **7:** National Library of Medicine (left), American Heart Association (right); **8:** National Library of Medicine; **9:** Bausch & Lomb (top), David Phillips/Science Source/Photo Researchers (bottom); **10:** Bausch & Lomb; **11:** NASA; **12:** Ontario Science Center; **13:** J-L Charmet/Science Photo Library/Photo Researchers (top), Thomas Alva Edison Foundation (bottom); **14:** Giraudon/Art Resource; **15:** National Library of Medicine; **16:** Pasteur Institute; **17:** University of Cincinnati Medical Center; **18:** Library of Congress (left), The Granger Collection (right); **19:** Bethlehem Steel Corporation; **20:** St. Meyers/Okapia/Photo Researchers; **21:** Library of Congress (left), Mary Evans Picture Library/Science Source/Photo Researchers (right); **22:** National Library of Medicine; **23:** Omicron/Science Source/Photo Researchers; **24:** Library of Congress; **26:** National Library of Medicine; **27:** Morgantown Energy Technology Center; **28:** Mary Evans Picture Library/Photo Researchers; **29:** Mary Evans Picture Library/Photo Researchers (top), U.S. Navy/Science Photo Library/Photo Researchers (bottom); **30:** Courtesy of the Archives, California Institute of Technology; **32:** The Granger Collection; **33:** Tom Dunham (left), UPI/Bettmann (right); **34:** National Library of Medicine; **35:** Tom Dunham; **36:** Pfizer, Inc; **37:** The Bettmann Archive; **38:** Cold Spring Harbor Lab Archive; **40:** March of Dimes Birth Defects Foundation (left), March of Dimes Birth Defects Foundation (right); **41:** University of Cincinnati Medical Center; **43:** Tom McHugh/Photo Researchers

Contents

Copernican Theory

Against the expert opinion of his time, a Polish astronomer discovered that the planets revolve around the sun.

Sunrise, Sunset

As you watch the sun "rise" in the east, "move" across the sky, and "set" in the west, it seems perfectly logical to assume that the sun is traveling around the earth.

Although several people before Copernicus had the idea of a sun-centered universe, it was not until the 16th century that others were willing to accept the idea.

And this is exactly what the ancients assumed. In fact, they believed that the earth was the center of the entire universe.

The problem with this thinking, however, is that it then becomes impossible to explain certain movements of the planets and to construct mathematical formulas to explain planetary motion.

A New Idea In 280 B.C., a Greek astronomer named Aristarchus, trying to measure the size of the sun, concluded that it was seven times larger than the earth. Although he grossly underestimated the sun's size, Aristarchus decided that the earth must revolve around the sun. The idea was much too radical for its time. Aristarchus was ignored.

Nearly two centuries later, Europe was in the midst of the Renaissance, a period of renewed interest in learning and new ideas. Into this era, Nicholas Copernicus was born.

The Revolution

Copernicus was born in 1473, the son of a wealthy Polish copper merchant and the nephew of a prince-bishop. No expense was spared on his education. In 1496, he traveled to Italy. He spent the next ten years there studying medicine, church law, and astronomy. In 1500, he attended a conference on calendar reform, which would, of course, involve thinking about the relationship between the sun and the earth.

By 1507, Copernicus was speculating that the sun-centered universe proposed by Aristarchus—and more recently by a German astronomer known as Nicholas of Cusa—made sense. For one thing, it would explain why the planets occasionally seemed to reverse direction when seen from the earth—moving west to east against the stars instead of east to west like the sun and moon. It also would explain why Mercury and Venus always stayed bright while the other planets grew brighter and dimmer. Finally, a sun-centered universe made the mathematics of planetary motions much simpler.

Copernicus went way beyond Aristarchus. In 1512, he began to formulate the mathematical details of his theory. His aim was to show how planetary positions could be calculated using the idea of a sun-centered universe. He hoped that even if people rejected his theory, they might find the calculations useful.

The Reluctant Rebel Copernicus was reluctant to go against the Catholic Church, which was committed to an earth-centered view of the universe. Therefore, for many years, he did not publish his ideas. Instead, he circulated them to other scientists in manuscript form. Finally, his friends convinced him to publish them.

This is an artist's interpretation of Copernicus's view of the universe in which the planets move around the sun.

His book, titled *Concerning the Revolution of Heavenly Bodies,* appeared in 1543. Copernicus dedicated the book to Pope Paul III in the hope of making it less offensive to the Church. According to one story, the scientist saw the first copy of his book as he lay dying from a stroke. However, that story was called into question when a copy of the book dated four weeks before his death was found.

A Theory for All Time Many scientists readily accepted Copernicus's theories. They began to base their own calculations on his assumptions concerning planetary movements.

However, as he had feared, the Church responded with hostility. Copernicus's book was placed on the Index, which is a list of books that Catholics were forbidden to read. It remained on the Index until 1835.

However, because of the printing press—invented around 1436—the book could not be repressed. Although it was very expensive, there were simply too many copies available for it to be ignored.

About 200 copies of the book still exist. Some of these copies are in private collections. The library at the Vatican (the headquarters of the Catholic Church and the pope's residence) has three copies of the book.

Today, many consider Copernicus's book to mark the beginning of modern science. It offered proof that the ancients did not know everything—that there were still things to be discovered.

▶ Copernicus's calculations helped later astronomers learn many things about the planets, including their distance from the sun.

Amending the Theory

Copernicus had made one error: he had accepted the ancient notion that planetary orbits were circular. During the latter part of the 16th century, Danish astronomer Tycho Brahe made detailed observations of planetary motions. After his death in 1601, his assistant, Johannes Kepler, tried to calculate an orbit for Mars that would conform to Brahe's observations. The numbers forced him to consider that planetary orbits might not be circular. In 1609, Kepler published his findings and his conclusion that planetary orbits were elliptical, not circular.

In the same year, Galileo Galilei first used a telescope to observe the heavens. By his observations, he confirmed Kepler's conclusions.

The View from Here To this day, after almost four centuries of careful and extensive observation of the heavens, our assumptions about planetary movements are still those of Nicholas Copernicus as amended by Johannes Kepler. They are not expected to change.

Distances of the Planets from the Sun	
Planet	**Distance**
Mercury	35,980,000 miles
Venus	67,230,000 miles
Earth	92,960,000 miles
Mars	141,000,000 miles
Jupiter	483,600,000 miles
Saturn	888,200,000 miles
Uranus	1,786,400,000 miles
Neptune	2,798,800,000 miles
Pluto	3,666,200,000 miles

Blood Circulation

An English physician discovered that blood flows through the body in a circular route.

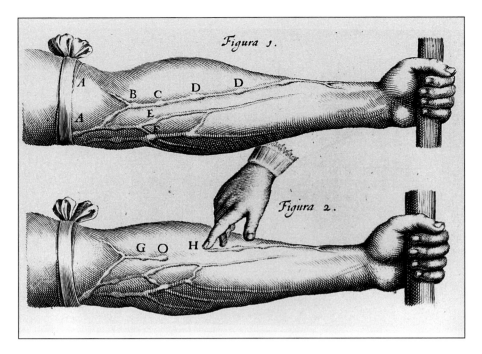

Harvey's work enabled physicians to control excessive bleeding caused by injuries by applying a tourniquet—a tight band placed around the injured limb (above the injury). We now know that tourniquets should be used only as a last resort and for a short time. Cutting off the blood to the injured limb can cause tissues in the limb to die.

An Old Question

One of the great thinkers of ancient times was Galen, a Greek doctor who lived in Rome during the second century. After many years of experimentation, which included the dissection of animals, Galen determined that arteries carried blood, not air. He also knew that the heart had four chambers: right and left atria (plural of atrium, meaning upper chamber) and right and left ventricles (lower chambers). However, Galen wrongly supposed that blood moved directly from the right side of the heart to the left side where it mixed with air. In fact, there is no opening between one side of the heart and the other.

Lesser Circulation In 1241, Syrian doctor Ibn al-Nafis observed what Galen had not: blood travels from the right ventricle to the lungs to pick up air. It then goes from the lungs to the left atrium, to the left ventricle, and to the rest of the body through a large artery called the aorta. Ibn al-Nafis correctly described what is called lesser circulation, the path the blood takes between the heart and the lungs. (It is called lesser circulation because it is the shorter of the two paths that blood follows.) Because of the lack of communication between the Middle East and Europe, Ibn al-Nafis's work was completely unknown in Europe until 1924.

However, there were Europeans who had described lesser circulation before that time. One such person was a Spanish physician named Michael Servetus. Unfortunately, Servetus and his books were burned at the stake in 1553. His discovery died with him. Then in 1559, Italian physician Realdo Colombo made the third discovery of lesser circulation and published a book explaining it. Although Colombo made his discovery several years after Servetus and more than 300 years after Ibn al-Nafis, his idea eventually became common knowledge among European doctors. Still, no one knew for sure what happened to the blood after it left the aorta.

One-Way Valves In 1574, another Italian surgeon, Girolamo Fabrici, made a discovery that helped answer the question of where the blood went after it left the aorta. While he was studying leg veins, Fabrici found valves in the veins that permitted the blood to move only in one direction—toward the heart. But Fabrici ignored his own discovery because it contradicted the accepted belief of the day—that blood coming from the left ventricle moved only away from the heart. The man who finally solved the mystery was William Harvey.

Putting It All Together

William Harvey was born in Kent, England (the oldest child of a wealthy businessman). After completing his education in England, Harvey went to Italy to study medicine under Fabrici. Harvey spent five years—1597 to 1602—at the University of Padua. There he studied the work Fabrici had done with leg veins.

Returning to England, Harvey continued doing medical research. He was especially interested in the heart and blood vessels. By dissection, Harvey discovered that the valves separating each atrium from each ventricle allowed blood to flow only in one direction: from the atrium to the ventricle and from there away from the heart.

Harvey combined this knowledge with Fabrici's discovery that veins forced blood to flow only toward the heart. He guessed that the heart pushed blood into the arteries and away from the heart, while veins brought the same blood back to the heart.

The Experiment Harvey needed a way to prove his theory. Soon he had it. Using animals, he first tied off an artery so that blood could not flow through it. The result was that the blood accumulated on the side of the artery toward the heart. The bulge in the artery clearly indicated that the blood was moving away from the heart. Then Harvey tied off a vein. The blood bulged on the side of the vein away from the heart. Harvey had his proof. Blood flowed away from the heart through the arteries and back to the heart through the veins. Blood had a double circulation: lesser (heart to lungs to heart) and greater (heart to other organs to heart). Greater circulation is so called because it takes a longer path than lesser circulation.

In another experiment, Harvey measured the amount of blood that the heart pumped out in one hour, he also showed that the blood that traveled through the body was not used up in the body. Instead, it circulated and recirculated, indicating a closed circulatory system.

The Last Puzzle Piece

Harvey published his findings in 1628. At first, many scientists ridiculed him. But his research was difficult to ignore. In his lifetime, most physicians came to respect Harvey's findings.

Until William Harvey, the ideas of Galen had been undisputed. But Harvey's experiments proved Galen wrong. Thus, Harvey has been called the founder of modern physiology, which is the study of the body.

There was, however, one unanswered question. Harvey had not been able to explain how blood went from arteries to veins. That mystery was solved shortly after Harvey's death, when more powerful microscopes became available.

In 1661, Marcello Malpighi examined bat wings under a microscope and detected tiny blood vessels connecting arteries and veins. He called them *capillaries,* from the Latin word for "hair." With the discovery of capillaries, knowledge about the circulatory system was complete.

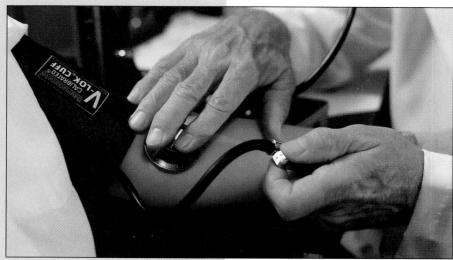

William Harvey (*left*) determined the amount of blood that the normal heart pumps each hour. Today, doctors use the same measurements to diagnose cardiovascular (heart and circulatory) problems. They use an instrument called a sphygmomanometer (*right*) to measure a patient's blood pressure.

Lenses That Magnify

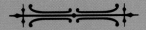

Lens makers found ways to make small objects appear larger and distant objects appear closer.

Ancient Spectacles

If you have ever tried to thread a needle or read the "fine print" on a legal document, you know how frustrating it can be to try to see something that is very small. That is why, for thousands of years, people have been working to develop better and better magnifying lenses.

Although we cannot know for sure, the ancients may have first noticed the phenomenon of magnification when they saw the surface of a leaf or a blade of grass enlarged by a dewdrop that clung to it. We know that the ancient Egyptians had a process for making glass and were capable of producing lenses.

Lenses, dating as far back as 2000 B.C., have been found in archaeological ruins in Asia Minor and Crete. They were probably used as magnifying glasses. The first spectacles, or eyeglasses, were made around 1280 in Pisa, Italy. They were convex lenses (lenses that curve outward). They allowed farsighted people to read more easily. Within a short time, reading spectacles were available throughout Europe. The makers of these spectacles were probably the first to notice that convex lenses magnify objects.

Tools of Modern Science

First Microscope In the late 16th century, the finest spectacles were made in the Netherlands. Therefore, it is not surprising that the next advances in lens making occurred there.

In 1590, a Dutch spectacle maker, Zacharias Janssen, had an idea. If one lens magnified objects, he reasoned, two would make them appear even larger. He placed two convex lenses at a distance from each other and found that magnification indeed improved. He, in fact, created the first microscope. Although the degree of the magnification was small, it was still greater than what was achieved by using just one lens.

First Telescope Soon after the first microscopes appeared, another Dutch lens maker, Hans Lippershey, had an apprentice who liked to experiment with the lenses he was learning to make. The apprentice found that if he held two lenses at a distance from each other and looked through both, a church steeple that was far away looked closer and upside down. When the apprentice showed his discovery to his master, Lippershey mounted the two lenses in a tube—creating the first telescope. That was in 1608.

Both the microscope and the telescope were essential to the development of modern science—the one enabling scientists to see smaller and smaller units of matter and the other enabling scientists to expand the horizons of the known universe.

◄ As the lenses for microscopes and telescopes were improved, scientists were able to learn more about the world because they were able to see so much more. This microscope was made in the 1700s.

From a tower in Venice, Galileo (*pointing*) demonstrated a telescope for several senators. The telescope was three times more powerful than any other that existed at that time. The senators were so impressed, they gave him a lifetime professorship and an increase in salary.

New Worlds Discovered

In 1660, Marcello Malpighi used a microscope to look at the tiny blood vessels (capillaries) that link veins and arteries. This discovery completed the work William Harvey had begun in describing the circulatory system.

Five years later, English scientist Robert Hooke placed a piece of cork under a microscope and saw chamberlike structures in the cork. He named the structures "cells." Eventually, scientists would discover that cells are the basic units of life.

Tiny Organisms Dutchman Anton van Leeuwenhoek was over 40 years old when he took up microscopy as a hobby. But he was soon to become the outstanding figure in the field. Instead of using two lenses in his microscopes, Leeuwenhoek used only one. But what a lens it was! His lens was so finely ground that it could magnify an object up to 200 times its actual size. This magnification was far beyond

any achieved to that time. In his lifetime, Leeuwenhoek would grind 419 of these exceptional lenses.

In 1676, while peering through one of his lenses at a drop of pond water, Leeuwenhoek was startled to see tiny living organisms swimming around in the water. For the first time in human history, people became aware that there were living organisms that were too small to be seen by the human eye. Leeuwenhoek called these organisms "animalcules." Today, we know them as microorganisms.

In addition to adding to human knowledge, Leeuwenhoek's discovery had medical benefits. It provided the foundation 200 years later for French chemist Louis Pasteur's germ theory of disease.

Making Improvements In 1609, just one year after Lippershey built the first crude telescope, Galileo constructed an improved model—building it in only one day. With his

telescope, Galileo was able to chart the mountains and the craters of the moon. He also was the first person to view the moons of Jupiter.

The first telescopes were refracting telescopes. The lenses curved light by refraction (or bending) and then focused it. However, there was a problem with refracting lenses. When lenses refract different colors of light, a rainbow of colors is formed around the central image and prevents the observer from getting a clear view.

In 1668, English scientist Sir Isaac Newton discovered a way to solve this problem by using curved mirrors instead of curved lenses. The resulting telescope is called a reflecting telescope.

Magnification Today The makers of today's powerful microscopes have abandoned the original principle of microscopes: that the observer views small objects directly. Ordinary microscopes use light waves to illuminate objects; the sharpness of the image depends on the light's wavelength. Modern scientists realized that electrons (negatively charged particles), which have shorter wavelengths than visible light, could be used to give a sharper image of smaller details. Today's electron microscopes can magnify an object up to two million times its actual size.

Using an electron microscope, this red blood cell is made to appear 2,000 times larger than its actual size.

The Theory of Gravity

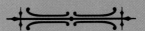

Sir Isaac Newton
saw an apple fall
to the ground and
formulated a central
law of nature.

Falling Down and Around

Drop an object and it will fall to the ground. But why does it fall down and not up or sideways? Aristotle, the ancient Greek philosopher, thought that he had the answer. He believed that the earth and the heavens were governed by two different natural laws. On earth, everything fell toward the ground. But in the sky, the sun, the moon, and stars moved in circles around earth. Thus, he concluded that the natural state of things on earth was to be at rest, while in the heavens, the natural state was to be in motion.

For about 2,000 years, this belief was commonly accepted. Then in the 16th century, Nicholas Copernicus proposed a sun-centered universe. In the early 1600s, Johannes Kepler suggested that the planets moved in elliptical orbits around the sun. Kepler's theory raised some questions. For one, what kept the planets in their orbits? The answer would soon come from an English scientist named Isaac Newton.

The Thinker Born in 1642, Newton was the son of a farmer who died before his son's birth. When his mother remarried, Newton was left with his grandmother to be raised on the farm. He attended school, but he did not care for classical studies. He was more interested in making gadgets and working models and in studying the world around him.

At the age of 18, Newton went to Cambridge University to further his education. Five years later, when the bubonic plague broke out in England, the university was closed. Newton returned to his family's farm. He spent the next 18 months thinking and developing the ideas that would make him famous. In the process, he laid the groundwork for a branch of science that would come to be called physics.

Newton developed calculus, the branch of mathematics that deals with the study of continuously changing quantities (essential for studying bodies in motion). He also did experiments on the nature of light.

Under the Apple Tree

One day, in the midst of all this mental activity, Newton was sitting in an orchard when he noticed an apple fall to the ground. He had no doubt seen an object fall many times before. But this time he started thinking about the force that drew objects to the ground and about the force that kept the planets revolving around the sun. (Although some historians maintain that this story is legend rather than fact, others say that Newton himself was the source of the story.)

Newton's thinking about falling objects eventually led him to the conclusion that all matter attracts other matter and that gravitational forces work at great distances between bodies in space. In other words, the very same force that pulled objects to earth kept the planets in their orbits. This was the law of universal gravitation.

Newton later worked out the precise mathematical formula by which the force between two objects could be calculated. According to this formula, the gravitational attraction between two bodies in space depends on how big they are and how far apart they are.

In addition to his theory of gravity, Newton contributed to many branches of science and mathematics. He is shown here studying the nature of light. Passing white light through a prism—a solid transparent object—creates a spectrum (Newton's term) of colors.

Write It Down! At the age of 24, Newton returned to Cambridge as a professor of mathematics. His work in mathematics and optics (he built the first reflecting telescope) brought almost immediate recognition of his genius. He was elected to the Royal Society—the oldest scientific society in Britain—at the age of 30. Surprisingly, however, Newton showed little interest in publishing his ideas about universal gravitation.

Then in 1684, astronomer Edmund Halley approached Newton with a question about planetary orbits. Newton answered Halley's question immediately but could not find the paper on which he had long ago worked out the mathematical calculation to support his answer. Halley urged him to write the calculation down again. Newton did so and presented his ideas about motion and gravity to the Royal Society in a paper called "On the Motion of Bodies."

Over the next three years, Newton expanded the ideas in the paper into his famous work, *Mathematical Principles of Natural Philosophy,* published in 1687. In this work, he explained his law of universal gravitation and his three laws of motion.

The Law Stands

Newton's laws were accepted without question. Only one thing marred his triumph. His longtime enemy, Robert Hooke, who had criticized Newton's theories about light, claimed credit for the ideas about gravitation. Hooke had proposed some ideas on the subject, but he lacked the imagination to formulate a theory as Newton had done. Nor did he have the mathematical skill to work out his ideas.

The scientific community of Newton's day adopted his ideas because they made sense. However, the theories were not proven until 1798, when English scientist Henry Cavendish did a laboratory experiment that verified the law of gravitation.

Later, in the 20th century, Albert Einstein modified Newton's laws. He did so to explain the motion of objects, such as electrons, that travel at close to the speed of light.

Newton's Legacy Isaac Newton effectively described the way the universe operates and showed how simple it is. His laws, as modified by Einstein, are still applied in the field of contemporary astronomy and the study of the motion of objects.

A body at rest remains at rest and a body in motion remains in motion at a constant speed and direction as long as outside forces do not interfere.

When an outside force changes the speed and direction of a moving object, the rate of change is proportional to the amount of force exerted.

For every action, there is an equal and opposite reaction.

▲ In order to launch a rocket into space, a great force is needed to overcome earth's gravitational pull.

◄ In 1589, Galileo began a series of experiments on falling bodies. Newton used Galileo's findings as the basis for his three laws of motion, which are stated here.

Electricity

Life has not been the same since Volta made electricity flow and Faraday generated it.

At the Ontario Science Center in Canada, a student demonstrates static electricity.

It Has Always Been Around

Look around your home, and count the number of appliances that run by electricity. Then try to imagine life without electricity. It would be very different, wouldn't it? Electricity has always been around. It just took several thousand years for people to harness its power.

About 2,500 years ago, a Greek philosopher named Thales was studying amber, a golden-colored glassy substance. Thales found that when he rubbed amber with his fingers, feathers and bits of cloth stuck to the amber. Today, we call this phenomenon static electricity.

Electrical Discoveries Over the years, scientists continued to experiment with electricity, which got its name in 1650 from *elektron,* the Greek word for "amber."

After much experimentation, Englishman Stephen Gray discovered that electricity could flow from one object to another. He also found that some materials helped it flow, or conducted it, and others did not.

Around 1745, Peter van Musschenbroek and other scientists at the University of Leyden in the Netherlands, began using a glass jar coated with tin foil to gather and store electricity. The metal coating helped conduct the electricity. When the so-called Leyden jar was packed with electricity, it could give quite a shock if handled improperly.

American scientist and statesman Benjamin Franklin also was fascinated by electricity. In 1752, he flew a kite with a metal key attached to it to show that lightning in the sky was the same force that was called electricity on earth.

Then in 1780, Italian scientist Luigi Galvani made an erroneous conclusion about electricity that set the stage for the most spectacular discoveries of all. Galvani was experimenting with Leyden jars. In the same room, he was doing an unrelated experiment with dead frog legs. When a spark from the Leyden jar caused a frog leg to twitch, Galvani was surprised. Electricity had made the dead muscles behave as if they were alive. He did further experiments with various metals and muscles and concluded that living things were full of electricity that did not disappear immediately after death.

Batteries to Generators

Alessandro Giuseppe Volta, another Italian scientist, was familiar with Galvani's work. However, he disagreed with Galvani's conclusions. Volta did not think that muscles had electricity in them. He thought that perhaps the electricity came from the metals Galvani had used in his experiments.

Producing a Current In 1794, Volta produced electricity in a different way. He used two kinds of metal (copper and tin) in salty water, which he knew to be a conductor of electricity. He experimented for several years. Then in 1800, he arranged a series of alternating copper and tin or zinc strips in bowls of salty water. When he joined the strips at the beginning and end of the series, electricity kept running through the circuit. Volta had created the first electric battery. (A battery is a group of similar objects working as a unit—such as the bowls and wires Volta used.) Until that time, all electricity had been static. That is, it stayed in one object. But Volta's electricity moved through wires. This new kind of electricity was called an electric current.

Using a stack of copper, zinc, and cardboard moistened with salt water, Volta produced electricity that moved—an electric current that flowed when two dissimilar objects were brought into contact.

Electric and Magnetic Scientists were aware of some similarities between electricity and magnetism. For example, both have opposites. In both cases, the opposites attract and the similars repel. There seemed to be a connection between electricity and magnetism, once thought to be two separate forces.

In 1819, Danish physicist Hans Christian Oersted discovered that a wire carrying an electric current acted like a magnet. Then in 1831, English scientist Michael Faraday showed that magnetism could produce electricity. By turning a copper plate around and around near a magnet, an electric current was produced in the copper.

At about the same time, in the United States, physicist Joseph Henry used electricity to turn a wheel, thus inventing the electric motor, a device with unimagined potential. All electric generators are based on the principles formulated by Faraday and Henry.

The Age of Electricity

The invention of the electric motor revolutionized the way work was done. Much of the work that previously had been powered by the muscles of humans and animals could now be powered by electricity.

In addition to bringing labor-saving devices into the home and the workplace, electricity revolutionized communications. Samuel Morse's telegraph (1844) and Alexander Graham Bell's telephone (1876) evolved because of electricity. Thomas Alva Edison contained electricity in a small glass receptacle—the light bulb (1879)—and the world became a brighter place.

Throughout the 20th century, the uses of electricity have multiplied. Today, a vast array of appliances use electric power—from toothbrushes and carving knives to bottle warmers and curling irons. People cook with electricity and cool their homes and businesses with electricity. They also process enormous amounts of information in computers, which would not exist without electricity.

In 1879, Thomas Edison and his associates produced the first successful electric light bulb. One of his associates, African-American engineer Lewis H. Latimer, developed the carbon filament used in light bulbs.

The First Medical Use of Ether

More than 100 years after its discovery, ether was used to eliminate pain during surgery.

Killing Pain Naturally

Imagine having a tooth wrenched from your mouth without anything to dull the pain. Imagine having an infected limb amputated with only a few gulps of alcohol to numb you beforehand. This is what surgery was like before doctors discovered the painkilling properties of ether.

The attempt to get relief from pain has a long history. Around 4,000 years ago, the ancient Mesopotamians knew that certain natural substances—opium, Indian hemp, and mandrake—dulled the senses and thus reduced physical pain. To obtain the same results, Roman naturalist Pliny the Elder used a mixture of powdered marble and vinegar. In the Far East, the ancient art of acupuncture—the insertion of very fine needles into the skin—was used to relieve pain.

Much later, on European battlefields, pain was relieved with a mixture of alcohol and gunpowder. And still later, in the 18th century, German doctor Franz Mesmer used hypnotism to render his patients insensitive to pain. Although scientists rejected Mesmer as a fake, his name lives on in the word *mesmerize*.

Painkillers from the Lab

Some early chemists knew about ether in the 13th century. But it was not produced in a laboratory for nearly five centuries. It was first produced by German scientist August Sigismund Frobenius in 1730. Still, no one thought to use it as an anesthetic.

However, in the same century, interesting effects of other chemicals were being discovered. In 1799, English pharmacist Humphry Davy was combining gases to produce nitrous oxide. He accidentally inhaled some of the mixture and experienced a feeling of great joy.

Davy was soon holding gatherings at which guests amused themselves by inhaling the gas. At the parties, Davy observed that people under the effects of the gas experienced no pain when injured. Davy tried to promote nitrous oxide, which today is called laughing gas, as a painkiller during surgery. He had little success. Many people felt that pain was unavoidable and that attempts to prevent it were unnatural and evil.

Although pain-reducing substances had been known since ancient times, they were not routinely used and surgery was a painful process.

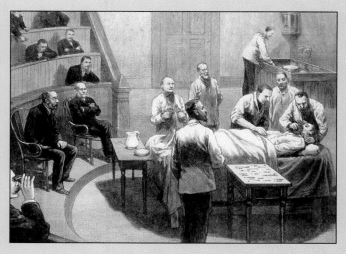

Doctors watched as Morton demonstrated the use of ether during an operation at Boston's Massachusetts General Hospital.

ANESTHETICS USED TODAY

Type of Anesthetic	Common Uses	How Taken
Benzocaine	To treat skin irritation, toothache, and teething pain	Ointment, cream, gel, liquid, spray
Lidocaine	To treat skin irritation, pain during dental treatment	Ointment, cream, spray, injection
Procaine	To relieve pain before surgical or dental treatment	Injection
Sodium pentothal	To induce and maintain unconsciousness, as during surgery	Injection into vein
Nitrous oxide	To induce and/or maintain unconsciousness	Inhalation

Ether Rediscovered

By the 1840s, people in the United States had rediscovered ether—as a recreational drug. They held "ether frolics" at which they inhaled the substance. One participant was a rural Georgia physician named Crawford W. Long. After experiencing the effects of ether, Long guessed that it might be used as a painkiller. In 1842, he used ether on a patient while removing a growth from the patient's neck. It was successful in killing the pain. Two years later, Long's wife became the first woman to deliver a baby while under the effects of ether. However, Long did not pursue his experiments with ether, nor did he publish his findings. By 1849, credit for the first use of ether as an anesthetic had gone to someone else.

The Ambitious Dentist Boston dentist William Morton had a dream. He wanted to eliminate pain during tooth extractions. He would not mind if he became rich in the process. When Morton learned about ether frolics, he began to experiment with the substance. He used himself and his dog as subjects.

On the evening of September 30, 1846, a music teacher named Eben Frost came to Morton with a severe toothache. He begged to be mesmerized so that he would not feel pain during the extraction. Morton offered him something better, and Frost accepted. Within minutes, Frost had been etherized, his tooth had been extracted painlessly, and he had regained consciousness.

When an account of the surgery appeared in a Boston newspaper, Morton was asked to demonstrate the use of ether at Massachusetts General Hospital. He did so a few weeks later, etherizing a patient who was to have a tumor removed from his jaw. After the 30-minute surgery, the patient proclaimed that he had felt no pain.

Boston's medical community praised Morton's discovery. But the unfortunate dentist was not to reap the benefits of his work. A jealous colleague spent the next several years trying to convince the world that he, not Morton, had made the discovery. Morton was driven to financial ruin and an early death. But the discovery itself was to prove valuable to many sufferers.

The first three anesthetics on this chart cause a loss of feeling in the area being treated. The last two cause a loss of consciousness and feeling.

The Age of Anesthesia

Morton's success with ether led doctors to experiment with other forms of anesthesia (a term coined in 1846 by Dr. Oliver Wendell Holmes from the Greek for "lack of feeling").

In 1847, Scotsman James Simpson began using chloroform as a painkiller. Later developments included the first use of a local anesthetic, one that would dull pain only in the area being treated rather than the entire body. Intravenous anesthetics, injected into the bloodstream, were first used in 1902.

The use of anesthesia changed the nature of surgery. With patients no longer writhing in pain, doctors had more time to examine patients' internal organs during operations. They observed that certain diseases were associated with changes in the internal organs and removed the affected organs. This practice contributed to an overall rise in life expectancy that continues today.

Germ Theory

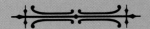

By proving that germs could cause disease, Pasteur laid the foundation for modern medicine.

Pasteur applied his knowledge of microorganisms to disease. His theory marked the beginning of modern medicine.

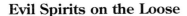

Evil Spirits on the Loose

Generations of parents have insisted that children cover their mouths when they cough and wash their hands before eating. Why? The answer is that today we know that germs (microorganisms and bacteria) spread diseases from one person to another, and that cleanliness can prevent this spread.

People have not always known about germs. For thousands of years, people had no idea about the causes of the diseases that afflicted them. Some people blamed evil spirits or foul air. Others said that diseases were God's punishment for sin.

Seeing the Unseeable A breakthrough toward an understanding of disease occurred in 1676. In that year, Dutch lens maker Anton van Leeuwenhoek constructed a microscope of such high quality that he could see tiny living creatures, or microorganisms, with it. At that time, however, no one knew that these tiny organisms could cause disease. But scientists now knew of their existence.

The Cure Before the Cause By the 1700s, people had begun to notice that if they came into contact with a sick person, they might become sick themselves. In the 1840s, Hungarian doctor Ignaz Semmelweis noticed that many women who had babies in his hospital became sick, but women who had babies at home did not. He considered the possibility that the doctors might be transferring infections from their sick patients to the new mothers.

Semmelweis insisted that physicians wash their hands in strong chemicals before tending to each patient. The incidence of infections dropped dramatically. Even so, the doctors did not believe that something invisible to the eye was causing their patients to become ill.

The physicians stopped washing their hands, and the incidence of infections at the hospital increased. But because Semmelweis was unable to prove his "germ theory," the doctors were unwilling to comply with his recommendations. Before long, however, someone else proved that Semmelweis had been on the right track. That person was Louis Pasteur.

To the Rescue!

In 1856, France's winegrowers were in serious trouble. Their wine was turning sour, and no one knew why. They went to chemist Louis Pasteur for help. Pasteur examined some wine under a microscope. He found several different types of yeast microorganisms in the wine. Some of them helped turn the grape juice into wine. But others caused the wine to sour. Pasteur recommended heating the wine to kill the harmful organisms. The winegrowers took his advice, and the wine remained drinkable.

Even after he had solved the winegrowers' problem, Pasteur continued to think about the sour wine. If harmful microorganisms could contaminate "healthy" wine, could they also invade healthy bodies and make them sick?

Linking Disease and Germs A few years later, Pasteur had his answer. In 1865, another French industry—the silkworm industry—was failing. Silkworms, a variety of caterpillar, live on mulberry trees and eat the leaves. People use the fiber from the silkworm cocoons to weave a lustrous and expensive fabric called silk. But France's silkworms were dying in great numbers, and no one knew why.

Once again, Pasteur was called in. Examining the mulberry leaves under a microscope, he found microorganisms growing in some of them. After finding the same microorganisms in the bodies of the dead silkworms, he concluded that microorganisms could indeed cause healthy creatures to become sick and die.

The Germ Theory Pasteur organized his findings into what is now called the "germ theory of disease." According to Pasteur's theory,

- Diseases are caused by harmful microorganisms.
- Microorganisms can travel through the air when someone coughs or sneezes.
- Microorganisms can travel from one person's body to another's.
- Microorganisms can live in the body's waste products.
- Diseases can spread from one person to another. These are called *contagious* diseases.

Saving Lives

Louis Pasteur's germ theory of disease was the beginning of modern medicine. Medical researchers began to identify the specific microorganisms, or bacteria, that caused various diseases. This information, in turn, helped them to develop preventions and cures for many diseases.

Pasteur's theory gained wide acceptance. Physicians began to teach their patients about the importance of cleanliness. In the late 1800s, English surgeon Joseph Lister encouraged doctors not only to wash their hands but to sterilize their surgical instruments as well. As expected, the number of patients dying from infections following surgery dropped considerably.

Lister's techniques gained acceptance in England, France, Germany, and the United States. Although modified slightly over the years, Lister's practices remain the basis for modern surgery throughout the world.

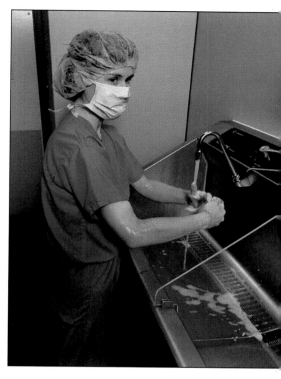

In addition to wearing face masks and specially sterilized garments, modern physicians scrub with antibacterial solutions before performing surgery.

Because of the work of Pasteur and Lister, fewer people die from disease and postoperative infections.

By identifying various types of microorganisms and the diseases they cause, medical researchers have been able to develop medications to cure the diseases and vaccines to prevent them.

LIFE EXPECTANCY AT BIRTH IN THE U.S., 1910–1990

Age (vertical axis): 45, 50, 55, 60, 65, 70, 75, 80, 85, 90

Year (horizontal axis): 1910, 1930, 1950, 1970, 1990

■ Male ■ Female

Source: U.S. National Center for Health Statistics.

SOME DISEASES CAUSED BY MICROORGANISMS

Cocci	Bacilli	Spirilla	Viruses
Pneumonia** Rheumatic fever Strep throat Tonsillitis	Diphtheria* Legionnaires' disease Salmonella poisoning Tetanus* Tuberculosis Whooping cough*	Lyme disease Syphilis	Influenza* Common cold Measles* Mumps* Chicken pox*

*Denotes the availablilty of a vaccine.
**Denotes the availablilty of a vaccine for some, but not all, strains.

Bessemer Process

A new method made it easier and cheaper to produce steel.

The Steel Problem

Since about 1200 B.C., people have recognized steel as the strongest metal. Until the 19th century, however, making steel was difficult and expensive. The situation changed after an English steel manufacturer tackled the problem. That man was Henry Bessemer.

An Urge to Invent Bessemer was the son of an engineer. From an early age, Henry Bessemer was interested in inventing. By the time he was 20, he had invented a new method of stamping official documents, which the British government promptly adopted—but without compensating Bessemer for his efforts.

However, Bessemer did not let this lack of payment discourage him from trying to help his country once again. In the 1850s, Great Britain, with its allies France and Turkey, was engaged in the Crimean War against Russia. Bessemer set out to develop a cannon shell that would revolve. By spinning as it was shot from the cannon, the shell could go farther and find its target more accurately.

Cannons of Steel When Britain expressed no interest in such a projectile, Bessemer took his idea to France. The French were impressed. However, they noted one important flaw. Unless the shell fitted tightly in the cannon, expanding gas produced by burning powder would leak past the shell and impede the force that was needed to set the shell spinning. What was needed was more, not less, pressure in the cannon. However, if greater pressure were exerted in the cannons of the day—which were made of iron—they would explode.

Bessemer knew that he had to find a way to make cannons of steel. Such cannons would be strong enough to withstand the increased pressure. But steel was too expensive to be a practical substitute for iron. Bessemer set out to discover a way to make steel inexpensively.

Although Bessemer's original purpose was to make a better weapon, he succeeded in creating a process that revolutionized existing industries and helped create new ones.

Cheap Steel

Steel consists of iron mixed with small amounts of carbon and other substances. The traditional way of producing steel involved turning carbon-rich cast iron into wrought iron (pure iron). Cast iron is hard, but brittle. Wrought iron can be made into any shape, but it is soft. By adding just the right amount of carbon, it becomes steel.

Bessemer's idea was to remove just the right amount of carbon from the cast iron and eliminate the wrought iron stage. He thought that he could achieve this aim by adding a blast of oxygen during the process. The oxygen would combine with the excess carbon to form carbon monoxide gas, which would then burn off.

Would It Work? Many people expressed doubts about the idea. They said that the cold air would cool and solidify the molten iron and stop the whole process. But Bessemer held fast to his theory.

Then he tried it. He found that the blast of oxygen did indeed burn off the carbon. Furthermore, instead of having the oxygen cool the iron, the burning carbon actually raised the temperature of the molten iron. As a result, an external source of heat was not needed. By stopping the process at precisely the right moment, Bessemer had made steel without going through the wrought iron step and with lower fuel costs. Cheaper steel was indeed possible!

Ironing Out the Kinks Bessemer announced his process in 1856. England's iron makers immediately invested huge sums of money in the "blast furnaces" needed for the new process. However, it soon appeared that something had gone wrong. The quality of the new steel being produced was very poor. Bessemer was denounced as a fraud.

Bessemer reviewed his experiments and the new steel-making process. He quickly discovered that the iron makers were using iron ore that contained phosphorous. He had used phosphorous-free ore, and that made all the difference. However, the iron makers were reluctant to trust Bessemer again. In 1860, he set up his own steelworks.

This engraving shows Bessemer steel production in the 1880s at the Carnegie steel works in Pittsburgh, Pennsylvania.

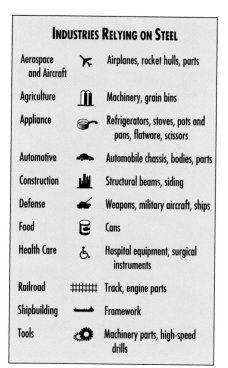

INDUSTRIES RELYING ON STEEL

Aerospace and Aircraft	✈	Airplanes, rocket hulls, parts
Agriculture		Machinery, grain bins
Appliance		Refrigerators, stoves, pots and pans, flatware, scissors
Automotive		Automobile chassis, bodies, parts
Construction		Structural beams, siding
Defense		Weapons, military aircraft, ships
Food		Cans
Health Care	♿	Hospital equipment, surgical instruments
Railroad	┼┼┼┼┼	Track, engine parts
Shipbuilding		Framework
Tools	⚙	Machinery parts, high-speed drills

Steel is one of the world's cheapest and most useful metals. It is used to make thousands of products—from paper clips to spacecraft.

The Age of Steel

Henry Bessemer's plant was so successful that, within a few years, he was a very wealthy man. Bessemer's process was revolutionary, but not perfect. In 1883, English steel manufacturer Robert Hadfield produced a steel alloy containing 12 percent manganese. This steel was very hard, and not brittle. Up to this time, ordinary steel used for railroad ties lasted only about nine months. Ties made with the alloy lasted 22 years.

Steel Goes with Everything The availability of cheap steel changed transportation and construction forever. Today, huge ocean liners, built of steel, carry passengers and freight

Fiery hot iron is poured into a furnace, blasted with oxygen, mixed with selected additives, and refined into steel.

from one continent to another. Towering skyscrapers, with their steel skeletons, crowd the city skylines. Majestic suspension bridges span wide rivers and bays.

Steel can be made so strong that it can support the world's tallest office buildings. It can also be made delicate enough to spin into fibers for rugs. Steel continues to be a remarkable and important material.

The Theory of Evolution

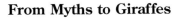

More than a century ago, Charles Darwin proposed a theory about the origins of life.

Lamarck's erroneous theory of the evolution of long-necked giraffes was based on the idea that acquired characteristics are inherited.

From Myths to Giraffes

For thousands of years, people relied on myths and religion to explain the natural world. For example, almost every culture and religion has its own version of the creation of the world.

However, some ancient Greek philosophers wanted to look at nature in a more scientific way. They tried to explain similarities between certain animals—such as lions and tigers—by saying that they might have descended, or evolved, from a common ancestor. The idea never took hold. Such a process would take a very long time. The earth would have to be very, very old for animals to have evolved from other animals. And as late as the 18th century, people believed, from reading the Bible, that the earth was only 6,000 years old. Not nearly enough time had elapsed for animals to have evolved.

However, in 1785, James Hutton, a Scottish physician whose hobby was studying rocks, found evidence that the earth was millions of years old. In fact, he believed that it was even older, but he could find no supporting evidence for when it actually formed.

First Theory of Evolution By this time, many scientists were beginning to suspect that biological evolution was a possibility. The problem was that no one could explain the mechanism that would account for the process. In 1809, French scientist Jean Baptiste de Lamarck proposed a theory of evolution based on the inheritance of acquired characteristics. Lamarck said that if one giraffe made its neck longer by stretching to reach the leaves at the tops of trees, then the offspring of that giraffe would inherit long necks.

Lamarck's explanation, however, was flawed. He was right that offspring inherit certain traits from their parents. But offspring do not inherit traits that parents acquire during their lifetimes. A short-necked giraffe that stretched its neck longer would still produce short-necked offspring.

Darwin Enters the Picture Charles Darwin was born in the same year that Lamarck proposed his erroneous theory. As a young boy in England, Darwin was interested in natural history. Later, to please his father, he studied to be a physician and then a minister. However, his real interest was always natural history.

Evolution Evolves

In 1831, Darwin was invited to be the official naturalist on the *Beagle,* a British ship that was going to sail around the world on a voyage of exploration.

For five years, as the ship made its way around the world, Darwin studied many plant and animal species. He was especially intrigued with the variety of life on the Galápagos Islands off the coast of Ecuador. For example, there were 14 different species of finches. Each species had a beak that was especially useful for obtaining food in the particular environment in which it lived. Some beaks were designed for cracking nuts and seeds. Others were good for scooping insects out of their holes. Yet to Darwin, the finches looked as if they might all have evolved from a common ancestor. But how?

Survival of the Fittest At home after the voyage, Darwin read a book by Thomas Malthus, an English economist. Malthus argued that the human population was increasing faster than food sources and that as a result not everyone would survive.

Darwin based his theory on the idea that nature "selected" those characteristics that made survival of the species more likely.

From this idea, Darwin concluded that only those most fit for their environment would survive and pass on their characteristics to their offspring.

Darwin applied this idea to the finches. Suppose that the original finches all looked alike. By chance, some finches might have been born with slight variations in their beaks that made it easier for them to obtain a certain kind of food. These finches would be more likely to survive. They would pass on to their offspring the beak shape that made survival more likely.

Darwin had the mechanism to explain evolution. He called it natural selection—the tendency of nature to select, or favor, those characteristics that promoted survival. He believed that it could apply to all living things.

Spreading the Word In 1842, Darwin wrote a 35-page essay on his ideas. However, he showed it only to friends. He disliked controversy, and he knew that his ideas would be unacceptable to many people. Darwin's friends urged him to write a book about his ideas.

He finally began the huge task in 1856. The book—*On the Origin of Species by Means of Natural Selection, or the Preservation of Favoured Races in the Struggle for Life*—was published on November 24, 1859.

In this cartoon, the artist expressed his dislike for Darwin's idea that humans and apes have a common ancestor.

Survival of the Theory

Darwin's book did provoke controversy. However, Joseph Hooker and Thomas Huxley, both eminent scientists in England, thought that it was outstanding. They offered to defend it against attackers. The book had plenty of critics, especially the clergy. They called Charles Darwin "the most dangerous man in England" and "the monkey man." This second name came from another idea in the book—that humans may have had a common ancestor with other animals.

Gradually, most scientists came to accept Darwin's theory of evolution by natural selection. However, even today, those who believe in a literal interpretation of the Bible still reject the theory of evolution.

For over a century, Darwin's theory has provided the basis for much scientific exploration. Two new scientific fields—molecular biology and developmental biology—are doing much to explain the similarities that all organisms have during their growth.

Genetics

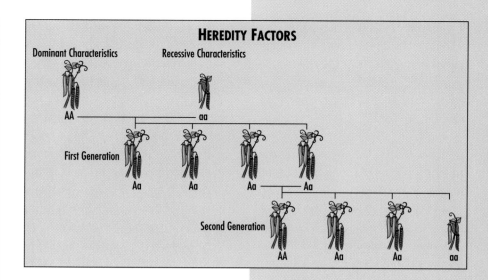

HEREDITY FACTORS

Dominant Characteristics — Recessive Characteristics

AA — aa

First Generation — Aa Aa Aa Aa

Second Generation — AA Aa Aa aa

Gregor Mendel lived a quiet life—mostly in a monastery in Austria—studying heredity in plants. Unfortunately, his enormous contribution to the field of genetics was not fully recognized until after his death.

Mendel's Failure

Have you ever noticed how much some of your friends resemble their parents? Perhaps they have the same eyes, nose, mouth, or body build. Throughout history, it has been obvious that offspring resemble their parents. But for most of human history, no one knew why. How people acquired their physical characteristics was not something that could be studied easily in a laboratory. But in the mid-1800s, an Austrian monk named Gregor Mendel unlocked the mystery of genetics.

Mendel grew up in a poor family, tending fruit trees on the manor of a local nobleman. After entering an Augustinian monastery in 1843, he was sent to the University of Vienna to study science and mathematics in order to become a teacher. However, Mendel was unable to pass the exam that would have given him the qualifications to teach in the advanced schools. He was appointed a substitute teacher at a nearby high school.

In 1857, Mendel decided to combine his knowledge of mathematics with his interest in botany. He would study the inheritance of physical characteristics using the pea plants in the monastery garden.

Mendel's Success

Mendel chose to study inheritance in plants since he could easily control the breeding of plants. A researcher can place pollen from one plant onto the pistil of another plant and produce seeds with two known "parents." This procedure is called cross-pollination. It is also possible to self-pollinate a plant. To do so, the researcher places pollen from a plant onto the pistil of the same plant. With self-pollination, the seeds have only one parent.

The Tall and Short of It For the next eight years, Mendel worked in his garden, pollinating pea plants in a variety of ways. In one study, for example, he worked with two different varieties of the plant: one that was quite short at full growth and one that was tall.

Mendel discovered that when short pea plants were self-pollinated, they always produced a short plant. Also, when tall plants were self-pollinated, they produced tall plants.

Then, Mendel cross-pollinated the self-pollinated short and tall plants. He wondered if some of the new plants would be short and some tall. Or would they all be of medium height? To his amazement, they were all tall.

Next, Mendel self-pollinated his latest batch of tall plants. Three-fourths of the resulting plants were tall and one-fourth were short. With these findings, Mendel was ready to formulate a theory.

Dominant and Recessive Mendel guessed that for each physical trait a plant had within it two factors—one from each parent—that determined the inheritance of a particular characteristic. These heredity factors controlled the eventual appearance of the plant offspring. He proposed that each characteristic had a "dominant" factor, which would appear in the offspring. Each characteristic also had a "recessive" factor, which the dominant factor would override.

In pea plants, for example, tallness was dominant and shortness was recessive. In the presence of one tall heredity factor plus one short heredity factor, shortness would disappear. However, in the next generation, the recessive shortness factor from one parent could combine with the recessive shortness factor from another parent, and the resulting plant would be short.

Rediscovering Mendel

In 1865 and again in 1869, Mendel published his findings in a small but respected scientific journal. The scientific world hardly noticed. Mendel was so discouraged that he stopped doing experiments. He died in 1884.

Then in 1900, three scientists working independently of one another—Karl Erich Correns, Erich Tschermak von Seysenegg, and Hugo de Vries—arrived at the same conclusions that Mendel had. Reviewing past articles on heredity, they uncovered Mendel's work and immediately gave him full credit for discovering the laws of heredity.

Chromosomes and Genes Mendel had formulated the laws of heredity correctly, but he had not known what the factors of heredity were. How did these factors actually work in humans? In 1882, German scientist Walther Flemming discovered chromosomes, rodlike structures in cells that duplicate themselves when the cells divide after fertilization. Chromosomes enable a cell to make an exact replica of itself.

In 1902, after the rediscovery of Mendel's work, American Walter Sutton discovered that the cells involved in human reproduction have only half the usual number of chromosomes. Thus, when a sperm and an egg unite, the resulting fetus receives half its chromosomes from its father and half from its mother.

Later scientists determined that each chromosome is divided into small beads. These beads control the inheritance of individual characteristics. In 1909, Danish botanist Wilhelm Johannsen gave the name *gene* to the individual beads on each chromosome. Then in 1944, American geneticist Oswald T. Avery proved that genes contain DNA. This is the chemical substance that transmits genetic information from one generation to the next.

Into the Future The rediscovery of Gregor Mendel's research sparked a flurry of investigation that is still breaking new ground. Today, genetic engineering—the splicing and recombining of genes from different organisms to produce new species—has been used to produce better crops. Through genetic engineering, scientists may one day eliminate many inherited human diseases.

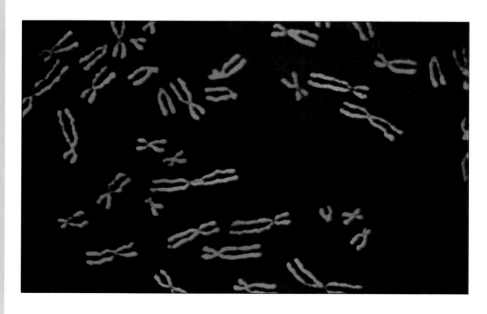

Chromosomes are rodlike structures that contain the genes that control the inheritance of individual characteristics. The chromosomes shown here are from human blood cells.

Periodic Table

A Russian chemist found an orderly way to arrange the known elements and to predict the discovery of some new ones.

Mendeleyev's organization of the elements was based on the principle that the properties of the chemical elements occur in repeating patterns.

The Elements

The ancient Greek philosopher Aristotle thought that the universe was made up of five elements. They were earth, air, water, fire, and ether (the heavens). For many centuries, scholars accepted this view.

Then in 1661, Irish chemist Robert Boyle published the modern definition of *element*. He said that an element was a substance that could not be broken down into simpler substances. Oxygen, iron, and carbon, for example, are all elements. In 1803, English scientist John Dalton said that elements are composed of tiny indivisible particles called atoms. Dalton later suggested that all the atoms of a given element have the same weight and size.

The Urge to Organize By 1863, scientists had identified over 60 elements. Chemists were busy trying to group them into families that would show the relationships among them. One of the organizers was English chemist John Newlands. His idea was to list the elements in the order of their atomic weight—the weight of one atom of the element. When he did so, he discovered that if he placed the first seven elements (by weight) in a row and the second seven beneath them, the two elements in each column had certain similarities. However, when Newlands tried to fit the rest of the elements into this scheme, he could not make it work. Newlands was on the right track, but he had not yet reached his goal.

Russian Chemistry The man who would eventually devise a workable scheme for arranging the elements was Dimitri Ivanovich Mendeleyev. One of 17 children, Mendeleyev was born in 1834 in Siberia, a vast rural area of Russia, where the government frequently sent prisoners as punishment. In fact, Mendeleyev's first science teacher was a political prisoner who had been banished to Siberia.

After Mendeleyev's father died, his mother took him west so that he could attend college. After studying at the University of St. Petersburg, he became a professor of chemistry there in 1866. He was considered one of the best chemistry lecturers in all of Europe. In 1868, he began writing a chemistry textbook.

The Order of Elements

Like Newlands, Mendeleyev thought about a useful way to organize the elements. He also began to arrange them in order of their atomic weight.

He soon noticed an interesting connection between atomic weight and valence. (Valence is the number of times an atom can form a bond—or chemical link—with another atom.) When he listed the elements by weight, there was an orderly rise and fall of valences. For the first seven elements, the valences went in the following sequence: 1, 2, 3, 4, 3, 2, 1. The second seven elements had the same rise and fall.

Furthermore, when Mendeleyev arranged the elements in rows so that the ones with the same valences fell beneath one another, the elements in the vertical columns had other similarities. Because there was a periodic, or regular, repetition of properties in each row, Mendeleyev's arrangement came to be called the periodic table. The order that governs it is called the periodic law.

Why It Worked Mendeleyev had succeeded where Newlands had failed. Instead of trying to make rows of the same length as Newlands had done, Mendeleyev recognized that the later rows had to be much longer than the first two. He also saw that a few elements, such as cobalt and nickel, had to be listed in the reverse order of their atomic weights for them to fall in the correct columns. This decision was proven correct more than 40 years later.

Filling the Gaps Mendeleyev published his periodic table in 1869. Although most scientists were unimpressed, the Russian chemist continued to work on the table.

In 1871, he announced that in order to fit all the known elements into his scheme he had been forced to leave gaps in the table. He predicted that new elements would be discovered that would fill these gaps. For three of the gaps, he described the properties of the undiscovered elements. Mendeleyev was proven correct when three elements, discovered in 1875, 1879, and 1886, did fill in the gaps and did have the properties Mendeleyev had described. The elements were gallium, scandium, and germanium.

The Table as a Tool

Eventually, scientists came to appreciate the importance of Mendeleyev's periodic table. Not only did it bring order to the list of elements, but it also guided scientists in their attempts to understand the structure of the atom.

Mendeleyev was shown to be correct even when he made exceptions to his own rules. In 1914, British physicist Henry Moseley proposed that an element's atomic number (the amount of positive charge in the nucleus) was the primary property of an atom, not its atomic weight. Mendeleyev's table still worked because the new theory showed why Mendeleyev had to place cobalt, nickel, and several other elements out of order for their atomic weights.

Mendeleyev Recognized By the 1920s, scientists realized that the periodic table was more than just a convenient way to organize the elements. The scheme made sense because it was determined by the fundamental properties of the atom. An expanded table, published in 1922, was virtually complete.

Dimitri Mendeleyev had died in 1906, just a few months after losing the Nobel Prize in chemistry by one vote. However, in 1955, a newly discovered element was named mendelevium in his honor.

The elements are arranged in horizontal rows according to their atomic number, which is the number of positively charged particles in the nucleus of one atom. Each atom has electrons (negatively charged particles) that spin around its nucleus in shells (groups). The numbers running down the right side of each listing refer to the number of electrons in each shell.

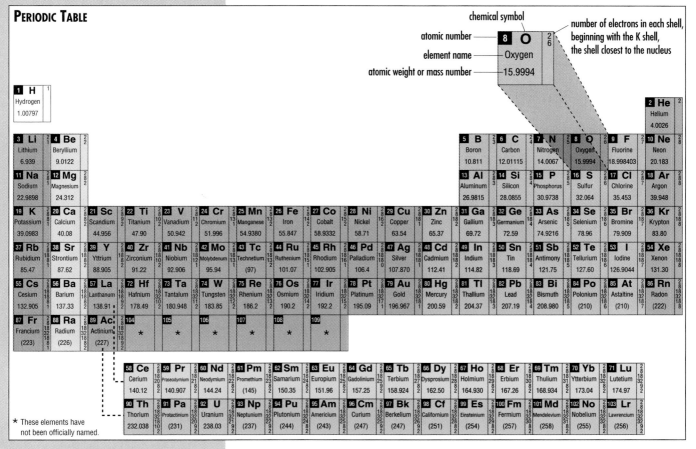

Quantum Theory

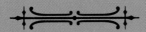

When Planck proposed the idea that formed the basis for quantum theory, even he did not believe that his idea was correct.

Max Planck gave scientists an important mathematical equation. But later scientists applied that equation to real phenomena and supplied the proof for Planck's work.

Several scientists applied quantum theory to explain the structure of the atom. Ernest Rutherford developed a model in which electrons orbit a small, positively charged nucleus.

The Black-Body Problem

In the late 1800s, physicists were puzzled. They had many laws to describe nature—theories about gravitation, magnetism, electricity, and radiation. But these laws could not explain some behaviors observed in nature.

Black Bodies One of those mysteries concerned the behavior of black bodies. A black body is a solid object, such as a lump of coal or a charcoal briquette, that absorbs all the light that falls on it. Because no light is reflected, the object looks black.

The German scientist Gustav Kirchhoff studied black bodies. He proposed that when a black body was heated, it should give off light at all wavelengths.

Here was the physicists' problem. There are many different kinds of radiation. Each is identified by its frequency and its wavelength. (High frequencies with short wavelengths include ultraviolet light and X rays. Low frequencies with long wavelengths include infrared light—plus microwaves and radio waves.)

There are many more high frequencies of light than there are low frequencies. Therefore, a black body should give off more high frequency light than low frequency light. But this did not happen. Physicists could not explain why. Then Max Planck thought of light in a new way. His new idea solved the mystery.

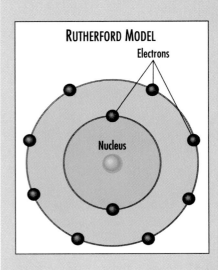

RUTHERFORD MODEL
Electrons
Nucleus

A Quantum Leap

Planck had been one of Kirchhoff's students. In 1900, he worked out a mathematical equation to describe how radiation is given off over a range of frequencies.

His equation was based on a new assumption. Physicists had thought that light was emitted in waves. Planck assumed that light is radiated in bursts or bundles rather than in one continuous flow. He called the bundles *quanta* (plural of *quantum*, from the Latin word for "how much?").

The Energy-Frequency Connection Planck said that the energy needed to emit a quantum of light was related to the light's frequency. The higher the frequency of light, the more energy needed to generate it. Violet light, for example, has a frequency two times that of red light. Thus, it takes twice as much energy to heat a black body enough to give off violet light than to radiate red light. To make the black body give off higher frequencies of light—such as ultraviolet—even more energy is needed. For that reason, a black body had never radiated light at these higher frequencies. The needed energy was not available.

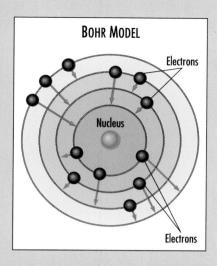

Electrons

Nucleus

Electrons

Planck's Constant Planck's equation was simple: *E=hv. E* stands for the energy of a quantum of light, and *v* is the frequency of the light. *H* is a specific number that does not change. It is called Planck's constant. Multiplying the constant times any frequency of light shows how much energy is required to make the black body emit light at that frequency.

Einstein's Aid Planck's view of light existing as bundles of energy was new and radical. Most physicists did not accept it right away. Even Planck wondered if his equation was a mathematical trick that did not really describe how nature worked. Albert Einstein, a brilliant physicist himself, helped show that Planck's equation was correct.

Einstein was the first to use Planck's equation. He applied it to what was called the photoelectric effect. Scientists had seen that when an object was struck by bright light, it gave off electrons, or negatively charged particles. The effect could not be explained when light was thought of in waves. Einstein showed how the effect made sense using Planck's idea of light as packets of quanta. By doing so, Einstein helped gain acceptance for the idea.

In Niels Bohr's model of the atom, electrons can move from a low-energy orbit near the nucleus to higher-energy orbits by absorbing energy. The reverse also is true.

Quantum Theory
Atomically Speaking In 1913, Planck's idea helped solve another scientific mystery. Physicists knew that an atom's electrons orbited around its nucleus. But they thought that the orbiting electrons should lose energy in their travels. As they lost energy, they should collapse into the nucleus. Scientists could not explain why this collapse did not happen.

That year, Danish physicist Niels Bohr proposed that the energy of an atom's electrons also must occur in quanta. Bohr said that electrons could add or lose energy only in full quanta. And he said that each electron had a lowest state of energy below which it could not go. That lowest state kept it in orbit. This theory explained why an electron could not collapse into an atom's nucleus.

Modern Physics Many other physicists began to build on these ideas. They developed a body of ideas called quantum theory.

Planck had proposed his theory of quanta to explain black-body radiation. He did more than that. His idea became the basis for a new physics. It so revolutionized how scientists looked at the universe that it became a dividing line. The study of physics before Planck is called classical physics. Physics after Planck is called modern physics.

Planck's theory inspired work in many fields and eventually led to the development of the laser.

Radioactivity

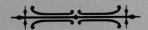

An experiment delayed
by cloudy weather
led to the discovery
of radiation and
nuclear energy.

The Unknown Rays

Radiation has existed since the beginning of the earth. But the first awareness of it came a little over a century ago.

In 1876, English scientist Sir William Crookes noticed a greenish glow in a glass vacuum tube through which electricity had been forced. The glow was later named fluorescence. It is caused by cathode rays, which are streams of negatively charged particles. These particles were later determined to be electrons—the negatively charged particles in an atom.

Then, in 1895, German physicist Wilhelm Roentgen was experimenting with fluorescence in cathode-ray tubes. He discovered that mysterious rays were emerging from the tube and penetrating a nearby sheet of paper coated with a salt compound, making it glow. He also noticed that these mysterious rays could pass through some materials (such as skin) but not through others (such as bone). Roentgen called his discovery *X rays* because *X* is the symbol for the unknown.

Impatience Rewarded

The discovery of X rays aroused the interest of French physicist Antoine Henri Becquerel. Several months after Roentgen's discovery of X rays, Becquerel decided to investigate the relationship between fluorescence and X rays.

Roentgen had produced X rays by stimulating metal with cathode rays. Becquerel wondered if he could produce X rays by stimulating fluorescent crystals with another source of radiation, sunlight.

The Experiment First, Becquerel wrapped a photographic plate in heavy black paper to prevent its being exposed to sunlight. Then, he placed a fluorescent crystal on the paper. Finally, he placed everything in the sunlight. His guess was that sunlight striking the crystal would cause it to emit X rays, which would penetrate the black paper and expose the photographic plate.

After leaving his materials in the sunlight for some time, Becquerel developed the plate. It was fogged. Becquerel was sure that the fogging proved that sunlight penetrating fluorescent crystals produced X rays.

However, being a careful scientist, he knew that he had to repeat the experiment to confirm his findings.

Unfortunately, just at that time, all of France experienced a long period of cloudy weather. Eager to do his second experiment, Becquerel prepared his materials. He wrapped the photographic plate and put the crystal on top of it. He waited days, then weeks, for the sunlight. Finally, he became impatient and decided to develop the plate. He hoped that the crystal had continued to fluoresce, even just slightly, during the cloudy weather and that there would be some fogging on the plate.

The Result To Becquerel's astonishment, the developed plate was more fogged than the first one had been. Even without the sunlight, the crystal had continued to fluoresce. The only possible explanation was that the crystal itself was producing radiation. This explanation turned out to be true. The crystal contained uranium, an element that scientists now know to be highly radioactive. Becquerel had been the first scientist to observe radioactivity in an element.

Becquerel set out to study the effects of combining fluorescence and X rays but discovered radioactivity instead.

The Curies are shown working in the laboratory. In 1906, when Pierre Curie died in a traffic accident, Marie was given his teaching position at the Sorbonne in Paris. She was the first woman to teach at that prestigious university. She was also the first woman to receive two Nobel Prizes.

Promise and Problems Today, the uses of radioactivity hold both promise and problems.

- Radioactive Dating: Because radioactive elements decay at a steady rate, it is possible to assign reasonably accurate dates to objects containing them. Scientists use radioactive dating to learn more about the earth's history.

- Nuclear Energy: Nuclear energy is an alternative to burning fossil fuels. However, radioactive particles from nuclear reactions can be extremely harmful. A 1986 accident at the nuclear reactor at Chernobyl, in the former Soviet Union, caused the deaths of more than 30 people and injuries to more than 500 people.

- Medicine: Radiation therapy, which uses radioactivity to destroy cancerous cells and tissue, is one of the treatments for cancer. Researchers are still trying to find ways to use radiation without its unpleasant side effects.

Radioactivity at Work

Fascinated by Becquerel's mysterious radiation, French physicist Marie Curie undertook a closer examination of the new phenomenon. Using a technique developed by her husband and teacher, Pierre, she set out to measure the intensity of the radioactivity. She discovered that the intensity of radioactivity was in proportion to the amount of uranium in the various compounds she measured. She was the first to use the term radioactivity.

Marie Curie also discovered two new elements that are more radioactive than uranium. She named one polonium, for her homeland, Poland,

and the other radium. For their work with radioactivity, Becquerel and the Curies shared the Nobel Prize for physics in 1903. Marie Curie won a second Nobel Prize—for chemistry in 1911—for her discovery of polonium and radium.

Later research in radioactivity led to Einstein's equation for the conversion of mass to energy and then to the atomic bomb and nuclear energy.

Theory of Relativity

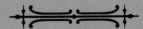

At the age of 26, Albert Einstein gave scientists a more accurate way of looking at the universe.

Einstein spent much of his life studying and developing theories of the universe that only a few people understood. He also enjoyed his relaxation. He is shown here riding a bicycle near his home in Princeton, New Jersey.

Thinking Things Through

After 1684, the theories of Sir Isaac Newton governed the way scientists thought about the universe. Newton based his laws on the assumptions that time, space, and mass were absolute, or non-changing. Scientists are always searching for "absolutes" or "constants" because these help to measure things that do change. Just over two centuries later, American physicist Albert Einstein proved mathematically that time, space, and mass are relative, not absolute.

Young Thinker As a child in Germany, Albert Einstein demonstrated little interest in school. He taught himself physics and mathematics so that he could ponder the subjects that interested him most: space and time.

The questions Einstein asked could not be answered in the laboratory, at least not with the technology of the late 19th century. He devised another method. He would ask himself a question and figure out a logical answer in his head. His questions and answers are called thought experiments. Then Einstein would do the mathematical calculations that proved his answers.

In 1901, Einstein received a degree from the Swiss Polytechnic Institute in Zurich. Unable to find a teaching job, he went to work in a patent office. He finished his work so quickly that he had time to do his thought experiments.

Frame of Reference

In 1905, at the age of 26, Einstein published four papers explaining his conclusions. Any one of the papers would have gained him recognition and respect. But the four together—and all in one year—astounded the scientific community.

The most famous of the four papers, titled "On the Electrodynamics of Moving Bodies," contained Einstein's theory of special relativity. In it, Einstein said that the speed of light (186,000 miles per second) is a universal constant. He also said that, from a stationary observer's point of view, a moving body changes as it approaches the speed of light. Its length decreases, its mass increases, and time measured on its clock passes more slowly than time measured on a stationary observer's clock. In other

Einstein's Life and Work

1879	Born in Ulm, Germany, on March 14
1901	Graduated from Swiss Polytechnic Institute in Zurich
1905	Publication of first papers, including paper on special theory of relativity
1915	Proposed a general theory of relativity
1921	Won Nobel Prize in physics for investigations of photoelectric effects
1933	Granted a lifetime professorship at the Institute for Advanced Studies in Princeton, N.J.
1940	Became a U.S. citizen
1949	Proposed a unified theory after 30 years of preparation
1955	Died in Princeton on April 18

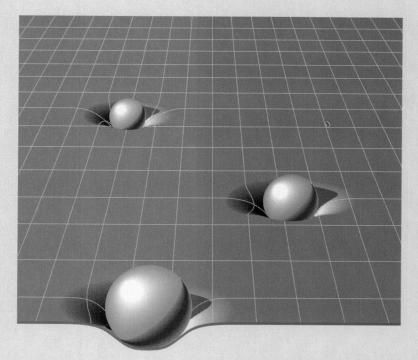

Large masses with strong gravitational fields (the globes) cause space-time (the grid) to curve around them. The greater the mass, the greater the curve.

The Triumph of Relativity

It took a while for scientists to grasp the complexity of Einstein's general theory. British astronomer Arthur Eddington was one of the first to fully understand the theory. When he was asked if it was true that only three people understood the general theory, he is said to have replied, "Who is the third?"

Einstein's theories of relativity have had some very practical results. By pointing out that mass and energy were related, Einstein paved the way for the creation, by scientists, of nuclear energy. Physicists could break up the mass of an atom and release energy. This is essentially what happens in nuclear bombs and nuclear power plants. Einstein regretted that his theory was used for making weapons.

The theory of relativity also has revolutionized humankind's view of space. It laid the groundwork for understanding black holes and the big bang theory. Black holes are the supposed invisible remains of collapsed stars. The big bang theory is the idea that the expansion of the universe began with a giant explosion billions of years ago.

Although Einstein demonstrated that Newton's laws are incomplete, they are still taught and still used to explain physical phenomena. In everyday life, at ordinary speeds, Newton's laws apply. Einstein's laws, however, enabled scientists to understand the world of subatomic particles (those smaller than atoms) that move at fantastic speeds and the larger world of the solar system and the galaxies.

words, all measurements are "relative" to the frame of reference of the person doing the measuring.

For example, imagine that you are sitting on a bus that is stopped in traffic. When the bus next to yours begins to move, it seems that you are moving backwards, even though you know that you are sitting still.

Most of us think that time passes in a regular way—that each second is just as long as the one before it and the one after it. But Einstein showed that at speeds approaching the speed of light, things begin to slow down.

This part of Einstein's theory was later proved using fast-moving particles called muons. Muons usually break down into smaller particles after about two-millionths of a second. But if they are made to spin at a speed approaching the speed of light, they take longer to break down.

Taking It Further Einstein's theory of special relativity proposed a new way of thinking about mass. Rather than being a physical object, mass is a highly concentrated form of energy. Einstein explained this idea with his famous equation: $E=mc^2$. The equation states that energy and mass are two aspects of the same thing. E stands for energy, m for mass, and c for the speed of light. To find the energy of a given mass, one multiplies the amount of mass by the speed of light times itself. Therefore, a very small mass multiplied by the speed of light times itself results in a great amount of energy.

The theory of special relativity dealt with bodies moving at an even speed. Next, Einstein wanted to extend his theory to apply to acceleration. In 1915, Einstein proposed his general theory of relativity. He theorized that gravity is not a force that acts directly across empty space between bodies. Rather, it is an apparent force that arises because space is distorted, or curved, in the presence of massive bodies. Therefore, bodies, particles, and even rays of light follow curved paths near massive bodies. This theory eventually gave scientists a better understanding of the effect of gravitation on astronomical phenomena, such as the movement of stars and planets.

Vitamins

These organic compounds are small parts of foods, yet they are essential to healthy life.

In 1772, James Cook commanded the H.M.S. *Resolution,* shown here. By providing his crew with a diet that included fresh fruit, he kept his sailors free from scurvy.

Mysterious Illnesses

Two centuries ago, life was very hard for British sailors. Living conditions on ships were rugged, and discipline was sometimes brutal. In addition, long sea voyages often resulted in a painful disease called scurvy. Sailors with scurvy suffered from a general weakness, bleeding gums, and muscle soreness. Many died.

In 1747, a Scottish doctor named James Lind discovered that sailors who had scurvy recovered when they drank the juice of citrus fruits (oranges, lemons, limes). No one knew why it worked, but it did. It seemed that fresh fruits and vegetables were necessary for healthy life.

More than 100 years later, the Japanese navy was having similar problems. A large percentage of the sailors had a disease called beriberi. A Japanese admiral compared his sailors' diet with that of British sailors. His men were getting fresh fruits and vegetables. But they were eating white rice instead of the barley eaten by the British. When the Japanese sailors were fed barley along with their customary white rice, the symptoms of beriberi disappeared.

Looking for Germs In the late 1800s, Louis Pasteur discovered that many diseases were caused by germs. Scientists began to look for the germs that they assumed caused scurvy and beriberi. They thought that perhaps the change in diet helped fight off the germs. However, no one succeeded in finding any such germs.

Breaking Down Food At the same time that some scientists were looking for germs that were not there, others were developing some very important theories about food. Chemists studying food identified five major components: carbohydrates, proteins, fats, minerals, and water. However, when they combined these components in the laboratory, the artificial food that resulted did not provide adequate nutrition to keep people from starving.

In 1870, France was at war with Germany. The city of Paris was surrounded by German troops, and Parisians were starving. French chemist Jean-Baptiste-André Dumas tried to make artificial food, but he failed. Something important seemed to be missing.

Something Missing Japanese sailors were not the only people afflicted with beriberi. In the 1890s, two Dutch doctors, Christian Eijkman and Gerrit Grijns, were studying beriberi among the people of what is now Indonesia. They noticed that chickens in the hospital yard that ate white rice exclusively were getting a disease very similar to beriberi. (White rice is what remains when the husks are removed from brown rice and the rice is polished.) When the chickens' diet was changed back to unprocessed brown rice, they recovered.

After failing to find germs or harmful substances in the white rice, Eijkman and Grijns concluded that the body must need something in the brown husk of rice. They decided that beriberi was caused by a deficiency, or lack, of some vital substance rather than by a germ.

Deficiency Diseases

In 1906, British chemist Frederick Gowland Hopkins became interested in the research of the two Dutch physicians. Hopkins had been studying scurvy, beriberi, and another disease called rickets, which caused children's bones to become soft and misshapen. He thought that each of these diseases was caused by a deficiency of a different substance found in very small quantities in food.

Hopkins was such a well respected scientist that his theory could not be ignored. Other scientists began to look for evidence that deficiency diseases were a reality. Scientists focused their efforts on beriberi.

"Vitamines" Then in 1912, American chemist Casimir Funk made an important discovery. He found that the substance that prevented and cured beriberi had, as part of its structure, a particular three-atom group. This so-called amine group contained one nitrogen atom attached to other atoms. Funk thought that there might be many different amines needed to keep bodies healthy. He called them *vitamines,* combining the Latin word for "life" with *amine.* When it later became clear that some of these substances were not amines, the word was changed to *vitamins.*

By determining the chemical structure of Vitamin C, and later of Vitamin B$_{12}$, Dorothy Hodgkin made possible the synthetic production of vitamins.

A diet rich in fresh fruits and vegetables can help people avoid certain deficiency diseases.

Viva Vitamins!

A year after Funk's discovery, American chemists Elmer McCollum and Marguerite Davis identified a substance in certain foods that prevented night blindness. McCollum and Davis called this substance Vitamin A and the anti-beriberi substance Vitamin B. Since then, researchers have identified and named many more vitamins.

In 1933, Vitamin C was synthesized, or produced in a laboratory. And in 1956, Dorothy Crowfoot Hodgkin determined the chemical structure of Vitamin B$_{12}$, which enabled it to be synthesized. Today, all vitamins can be produced in laboratories. These manufactured vitamins are used to enrich processed foods. They also are used to make vitamin-supplement pills.

Life Changers The knowledge of vitamins changed the way people cooked and ate their food. As a result, children today are taller and stronger than their ancestors were 50 or 100 years ago. Vitamins have made people healthier and increased their life expectancy.

Insulin

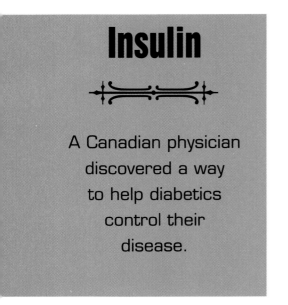

A Canadian physician discovered a way to help diabetics control their disease.

Searching for a Cure

Nearly 15 million Americans have diabetes, and about 30 percent of them have the disease without knowing it. Diabetes prevents the body from processing sugars and other carbohydrates properly. In severe cases, diabetics (people with the disease) are susceptible to frequent infections, weight loss, and damage to eyes, blood vessels, and nerves. People have suffered from diabetes since ancient times. Until the 20th century, those who had it died a slow, certain death, and no one knew why.

Examining the Pancreas The pancreas is the gland that produces certain substances that are needed for digesting proteins. In 1869, German physician Paul Langerhans identified clusters of cells in the pancreas that were later named the *islets of Langerhans*. These clusters of cells would play an important role in unraveling the mystery of diabetes.

Then in 1889, German researchers Oskar Minkowski and Joseph von Mering removed the pancreas of a dog. To their surprise, the dog developed symptoms of diabetes. Next they left the pancreas in another dog but tied off the tube that led to the duodenum (where part of the digestive process occurs). The second dog did not develop diabetes, but had some digestive problems.

A French researcher known as Hédon elaborated on the German researchers' experiments and concluded that the pancreas has two roles: one in the digestion of proteins and one in the processing of carbohydrates. In 1901, American researcher Eugene Opie confirmed that destruction of the islets of Langerhans brought about diabetes.

Scientists guessed that the islets produced a substance that aided in the processing of carbohydrates. They called that substance—*insulin,* from the Latin word for "island." If they could isolate insulin in an animal's pancreas, perhaps they could use it to treat human diabetics. But attempts to isolate the substance failed, and all efforts ceased—until one night in 1920, when a Canadian doctor had trouble falling asleep.

After serving in World War I, Dr. Frederick Banting returned to Canada where he became interested in the research that had been done on diabetes. Banting knew that scientists had tried to extract insulin from the pancreas. Before they could do so, however, digestive juices in the pancreas broke down the insulin. The problem, then, was how to isolate the islets of Langerhans from the rest of the pancreas.

After much trial and error, Banting and Best succeeded in isolating insulin. But before they used it on a human patient, they tried it successfully with animals.

Doctor Banting's Sleepless Night

To while away the hours during his sleepless night, Dr. Banting began to read an article in a medical journal. The article described an autopsy in which stones in the pancreas had blocked the pancreatic duct that led from the pancreas to the duodenum. Most of the pancreas had wasted away, but the islets had remained healthy!

The idea struck Banting: here was a way to isolate insulin. If he could tie off the pancreatic ducts of animals and wait for the gland to deteriorate, he would have healthy islets of Langerhans. The insulin extracted from these glands could be used to treat human beings with diabetes, thus relieving their symptoms and prolonging their lives.

A Sponsor Banting took his theory to the scientists at the University of Toronto to have it tested. He was able to persuade Professor John J. R. Macleod to give him laboratory space and a research assistant.

In the summer of 1921, while Macleod was on vacation, Banting and his assistant, Charles Best, conducted several experiments and succeeded in isolating insulin. Macleod provided Banting and Best with another collaborator, James Collip. Collip was the first to notice insulin shock—the body's negative response to too much insulin. Collip also devised a method for preparing insulin that enabled it to be injected safely into human beings.

By January 1922, Banting and his colleagues were ready to test their work on human subjects. They gave the first dose of insulin to a young boy, Leonard Thompson, who was dying from diabetes. Thompson recovered, and diabetes became a treatable illness.

Type I diabetes affects one in ten people. Because they need insulin on a regular basis, diabetics are taught to inject themselves, using a syringe.

Acclaim and Anger

Banting's work also laid the foundation for later research to determine the causes of the disease and to clarify the way the body processes carbohydrates and fats.

In 1923, Banting and Macleod were awarded the Nobel Prize for medicine. Banting was outraged that Macleod, who had merely sponsored the research, was included, while Charles Best was not honored. Banting generously shared his prize money with Best. Macleod shared his prize money with James Collip.

There was however, some additional controversy. A Rumanian researcher, Nicholas Paulesco, protested that he had published results of tests similar to Banting's in 1921. But the Nobel jury gave no recognition to his achievement.

The isolation of insulin improved the lives of diabetics and increased their life expectancy. Today, insulin is still the main treatment for those suffering from diabetes.

Diabetes was once an illness that meant certain death. Today, people with diabetes can live long and relatively normal lives.

FACTS ABOUT DIABETES

Type	Symptoms	Incidence	Complications	Treatment
Type I (Insulin dependent)	Excessive urination; excessive thirst; sugar in urine; sudden loss of weight	Usually under age 40	Vision problems; poor circulation to legs; increased infections; tooth decay; miscarriages; kidney disease; diabetic coma; insulin shock	Special diet; exercise; insulin
Type II (Non-insulin dependent)	Skin infections; slow healing; itching; tingling and numbness in hands and feet	Usually over age 40	Same as for Type I with exception of insulin shock	Special diet; exercise; regular medication

Penicillin

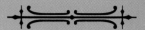

A "miracle" drug
known in ancient times
was rediscovered
three times before
modern medicine
took it seriously.

A Moldy Cure

In the ancient world, people were susceptible to many diseases. One particularly uncomfortable disease caused the victim's head to become covered with scabs. Fortunately, this condition could be treated—with magic incantations, potions of hippopotamus fat, and then rubbing the head with moldy wheat bread (an early form of penicillin). Early Egyptian physicians

The carelessness of a laboratory assistant led to the growth of a mold that opened a new era in the treatment of many diseases.

recorded these and other useful cures. But later doctors ignored them, regarding these cures as not sufficiently "scientific."

Centuries Later Many thousands of years later, in 1871, Joseph Lister was searching for a substance that would kill harmful bacteria more effectively than the known antiseptics, or germ killers. While attempting to grow in the laboratory the bacteria that caused cholera, typhus, and yellow fever, he came up instead with a fine covering of bacteria. He identified this "growth" as a mold called penicillium. In a later experiment, Lister added specific bacteria to the penicillium and noticed that the germs he grew on a thin layer of penicillium remained strong and healthy. But those he added to a thick layer of penicillium seemed unable to reproduce themselves. Lister, however, ignored the implications of these findings.

Years Go By More than 20 years after Lister's experiments, Ernest Duchesne, a teacher at the French Army Medical Academy, was experimenting with penicillium. As he worked, the famous words of Louis Pasteur—"life hinders life"—came to him. Testing Pasteur's idea, Duchesne added some bacteria to the mold. Within a few hours, all of the added bacteria had died. Duchesne then injected laboratory mice with deadly bacteria. Next he injected half of those mice with penicillium. The mice that did not receive the penicillium died, and the others lived.

For the second time, penicillium had been shown to fight bacteria. Again no one, including Duchesne, had any interest in continuing the research. The man who would finally "discover" penicillin—the miracle drug—was Alexander Fleming.

Third Time's the Charm

Alexander Fleming was born in Scotland in 1881. After spending five tedious years as a shipping clerk, he won a scholarship to medical school. During World War I, he served in the British army. There he became interested in finding an antiseptic that would kill harmful bacteria without damaging living tissue.

In 1928, Fleming was studying staphylococcus bacteria. He placed the bacteria in several petri dishes (small glass containers used in laboratories). He left to an assistant the job of covering the dishes and putting them in a cabinet where the bacteria would be heated to human body temperature. The next day,

By the end of World War II, penicillin was widely used to treat wounded soldiers. The so-called miracle drug saved many lives on the battlefield.

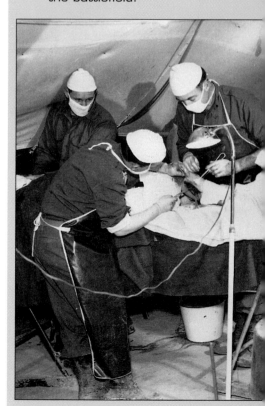

Fleming discovered that the assistant had failed to cover one of the dishes properly, and in that dish a gray-green mold had contaminated the broth in which the bacteria were growing. Fleming was about to throw the whole thing down the drain, when he noticed something startling. The mold was eating away at the bacteria! He called the mold *penicillin,* a by-product of penicillium.

Unlike Lister and Duchesne, Fleming saw great potential in his discovery. He continued to grow penicillin from the original batch and to test it on a variety of bacteria. Eventually, he discovered that penicillin could kill streptococcal bacteria, which caused such deadly diseases as diphtheria, tetanus, and influenza.

Despite his encouraging findings, Fleming was hesitant to try penicillin on human beings. Instead, he used penicillin to identify different kinds of bacteria that were not sensitive to it.

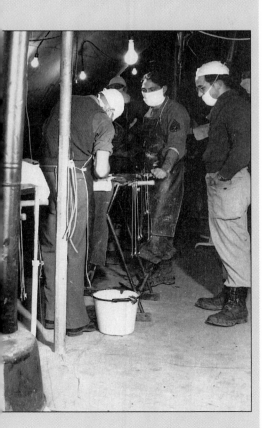

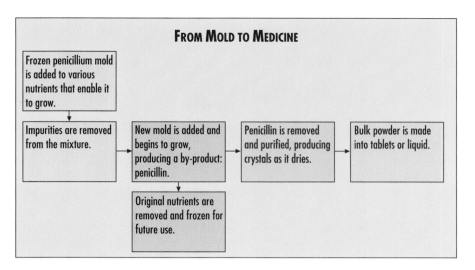

FROM MOLD TO MEDICINE

Frozen penicillium mold is added to various nutrients that enable it to grow.

↓

Impurities are removed from the mixture. → New mold is added and begins to grow, producing a by-product: penicillin. → Penicillin is removed and purified, producing crystals as it dries. → Bulk powder is made into tablets or liquid.

Original nutrients are removed and frozen for future use.

Since even the smallest impurities can spoil the batch, quality control checks are made at every stage of the process.

The Wonder Drug

Taking It Further In 1939, British scientists Howard Florey and Ernst Chain took up where Fleming had left off. They succeeded in producing a form of penicillin that could be used to treat human beings.

In 1941, while World War II raged in Europe, Florey left England for the United States to continue the research on penicillin. By 1943, penicillin was ready to be used on a large scale.

Saving Lives Toward the end of the war, penicillin was used to treat infections in wounded soldiers. In 1945, Fleming, Florey, and Chain shared the Nobel Prize for medicine. At that time, penicillin still had to be "grown" in laboratories—a complicated process. However, in 1949, British physicist Dorothy Crowfoot Hodgkin determined the molecular structure of penicillin, which made it possible to produce the powerful drug synthetically.

Its Importance Continues The chances are good that unless a person is allergic to penicillin, he or she will be treated with penicillin at some time. The drug is known to destroy 89 different disease-causing bacteria and to have some positive effect on 16 others.

Alexander Fleming once predicted that penicillin would save thousands of lives. That was a conservative estimate. It has probably already saved millions of lives, and its usefulness, in newer and stronger forms, continues to this day.

CONDITIONS TREATED WITH PENICILLIN

Abscesses	Pneumonia
Bronchitis	Rheumatic fever
Burns	Scarlet fever
Diphtheria	Sinusitis
Gonorrhea	Strep throat
Influenza	Syphilis
Meningitis	Tetanus
Otitis media	Tonsillitis
Peritonitis	Wounds

Penicillin—in both its natural and synthetic forms—is one of the most widely used antibacterial drugs. These are a few of the diseases it cures.

DNA

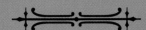

A century after Mendel
discovered the
laws of heredity,
scientists learned what
enables parents
to pass on traits
to their offspring.

- In 1879, German scientist Albrecht Kossel began to study the structure of nucleic acid. He isolated five substances in nucleic acid. He knew that the sixth was a sugar, but he did not know which sugar.

- In 1882, another German scientist, Walther Flemming, identified rodlike structures contained in all cells, which he called *chromosomes.*

- In 1909, scientists realized that chromosomes carried a person's hereditary makeup. Somehow, chains of chromosomes from each parent came together in an offspring. That same year, the individual units that made up the chains of chromosomes were named *genes.*

- Also in 1909, American chemist Phoebus Levene identified the sugar in one variety of nucleic acid as ribose. The acid was then named *ribonucleic acid (RNA).*

- In 1929, Levene identified the sugar in the other acid as deoxyribose. This acid was then named *deoxyribonucleic acid, or DNA.*

- At about the same time, Frederick Griffith, Jr., discovered that a gene from a dead pneumonia bacterium could reproduce itself in another strain of the bacterium that lacked that gene. Scientists called this the transforming principle and set about trying to identify it. They suspected that it might have something to do with heredity.

- Ten years later, Swedish scientist Torbjorn Caspersson found DNA in chromosomes. He concluded that DNA was involved in heredity.

A Maze of Discoveries

One of the most popular films of 1993 was *Jurassic Park.* Its plot is based on the idea that dinosaurs could be recreated from ancient DNA. The DNA is found in mosquitoes that bit dinosaurs millions of years ago. The mosquitoes were then trapped in amber, and thus the blood they had sucked from the dinosaurs was preserved.

But what exactly is DNA? And how did scientists find out about it? The answers involve a sequence of discoveries that ended by the 1940s.

- In 1865, Gregor Mendel—who had studied several generations of pea plants in his garden—proposed the laws of heredity. These principles explain that each individual inherits characteristics from both parents. However, Mendel had no idea what mechanism enabled this inheritance to occur.

- In 1869, Swiss biologist Johann Miescher isolated a substance inside the cell's nucleus. He called it *nuclein,* but he did not know what it did. He later named it *nucleic acid* because it had acidic characteristics.

In 1962, James Watson (*left*) and Francis Crick (*right*) won the Nobel Prize for describing the structure of DNA.

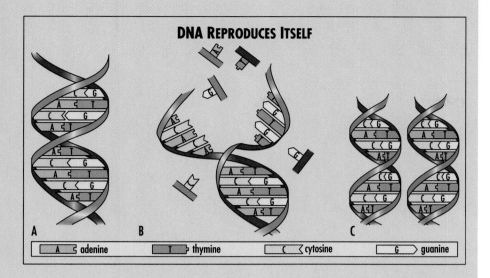

DNA REPRODUCES ITSELF

| A | adenine | T | thymine | C | cytosine | G | guanine |

(A) The intact DNA segment contains four types of nucleotides (building blocks): *adenines, thymines, guanines,* and *cytosines.* (B) The bonds between the two strands of the double helix weaken and separate; free nucleotides bond to the exposed strands. (C) Two new (exact copies) double helixes are formed.

The Maze Unraveled

For almost 15 years, scientists had been looking for the transforming principle, which enabled a gene to reproduce itself. In 1944, they found it. American bacteriologist Oswald Avery, working with Colin McLeod and Maclyn MacCarthy, isolated the transforming principle and identified it as DNA. They concluded that probably all genes were made up of DNA. They said that DNA carried the "blueprint" for inherited characteristics that were passed on from one generation to the next.

The Double Helix Having decided that DNA determined heredity, scientists then asked themselves, "What is special about the DNA molecule that allows it to multiply itself during reproduction and still keep the blueprint intact in the new cell?"

In the early 1950s, Englishman Francis Crick and American James Watson were trying to determine the structure of DNA. In another laboratory, Maurice Wilkins had prepared pure DNA fibers that would photograph very well. Chemist Rosalind Franklin photographed Wilkins's specimens. They were the best photos of DNA ever taken.

But Franklin was cautious; she wanted to study the photos. Without her permission, Wilkins showed the photos to Crick and Watson. Less cautious than Franklin, they concluded from the photos that DNA was a double chain. Each side of the chain contained nucleotides (the basic unit of nucleic acid) that were linked to the other side by a weak bond. The two chains could be joined or pulled apart like the two sides of a zipper. The two chains twisted to form a double helix (spiral). The double helix looked something like a pair of spiral staircases with a banister fitting between them.

Heredity Explained As described by Crick and Watson in 1953, the double helix structure explained how the DNA molecule produces copies of itself when it divides during reproduction. As a cell divides, the two strands of the double helix pull apart. Each strand picks up the material that it is now missing—the complementary strand—from fluid in the cell. Soon two new double helixes are formed. Each is an exact copy of the original. Thus, DNA reproduces itself without any changes in its structure.

DNA Today

The understanding of DNA has had a profound effect on modern life. By 1970, scientists had learned how to cut a molecule of DNA at certain locations and form fragments that could recombine with one another. The process, called recombinant DNA, or gene splicing, produces new genes that did not exist before.

Recombinant DNA led to genetic engineering, which enables genes to be changed, moved around, or even created. Through genetic engineering, scientists have been able to make bacteria that produce insulin and bacteria that turn pollutants into harmless fluids. They have been able to create new strains of food crops that resist disease.

In addition, the new understanding of DNA has enabled scientists to predict whether a baby will have certain hereditary diseases or birth defects.

Genetic engineering also creates dangers. Increased control of inheritance raises ethical questions about the amount of control humans should exert over nature. Governments are trying to establish safeguards to keep gene splicing from becoming harmful, such as by the accidental production of dangerous and uncontrollable bacteria.

Polio Vaccine

Two physicians produced vaccines that wiped out a dreaded childhood disease.

The Deadly Virus

Mention polio to anyone who was a child or a parent in the early 1950s, and see what the reaction is. At that time, poliomyelitis (also called infantile paralysis) was one of the most dreaded childhood diseases in the United States. In 1952, a record

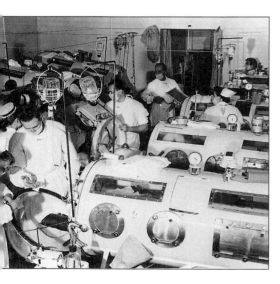

In the early 1950s, tens of thousands of people were kept alive by pumps in iron lungs.

number of polio cases—58,000—were reported in the United States.

Polio has both mild and severe strains. The more severe strains can cause permanent paralysis. Patients must use a wheelchair or leg braces and crutches for the rest of their lives. Others are confined to an iron lung—a large metal tubelike device that enables the patient to breathe.

Enders Takes the First Step

In the early 1950s, there was no known treatment for polio and no vaccine against it. The reason was that polio is caused by a virus rather than a bacterium. Viruses grow and reproduce only within other living cells, and thus they are difficult to study. While bacteria can be kept alive in petri dishes, viruses have to be maintained in a live organism. It is possible to grow viruses in embryonic tissue, such as chicken eggs. However, bacteria also can grow in embryos and mask the virus.

The first step toward fighting polio was to find a way to study the virus in a laboratory. In 1948, American biologist John Enders took that step when he developed a technique for using penicillin to prevent the growth of bacteria without interfering with the growth of the virus. Enders himself used this technique to develop a vaccine for measles, another dreaded childhood viral disease.

Salk Takes Up the Cause

The man who would use Enders's technique to develop a polio vaccine was Jonas Edward Salk. Born in New York City in 1914, the child of a Jewish immigrant from Poland, Salk became a physician in 1939. In 1947, he was appointed head of the Virus Research Laboratory at the University of Pittsburgh's School of Medicine. There he began his research on polio.

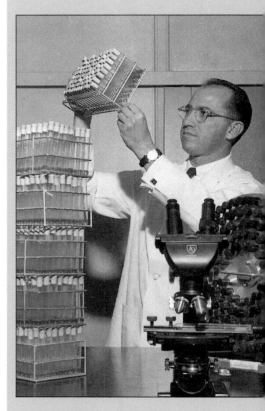

Dr. Jonas Salk, developer of the first polio vaccine, is shown here in his laboratory at the University of Pittsburgh.

Killing the Virus

Salk knew that a polio vaccine had to contain enough of the virus to produce antibodies—agents in the body that fight disease—but not enough to actually produce the disease.

Using the technique developed by Enders, Salk grew three different strains of the polio virus. Then for several days, he treated each of the strains with formaldehyde, a poisonous chemical. Formaldehyde is used mainly as a disinfectant to kill harmful germs and as a preservative. Salk's aim was to kill the viruses so that when they were injected into the human body, they would not produce polio. However, he wanted to leave them intact enough to produce antibodies that would make the body immune to the disease.

The Trials Salk first tested his vaccine on monkeys. The results were promising. The monkeys did not develop polio, but they did develop antibodies against the disease.

The next cautious step was to try out the vaccine on children who had polio and thus would not be further endangered if the vaccine was too strong. These tests also showed an increase in the level of polio antibodies in the children's bodies.

Still hesitant, Salk tried out the vaccine on members of his own family who had not had polio. Again, the results were what Salk had hoped for. Finally, Salk was willing to take the big risk. In 1954, he supervised large-scale testing of the vaccine on nearly two million American children. The vaccine had a success rate of more than 80 percent. (With any vaccine, there is always a risk factor that can cause some people to contract the disease.)

When the tests were completed, the vaccine was immediately made available to the general public. Because of the rush to protect as many children as possible as fast as possible, Salk gave a number of companies the instructions for making the vaccine. When some improperly prepared vaccine led to several hundred cases of polio, the entire vaccination program nearly ended. However, the cause of the problem was discovered and remedied, and the program continued.

Polio has been virtually wiped out in the developed countries of the world. To eliminate the disease completely would take a global vaccination program.

Dr. Sabin, shown here, developed a longer-lasting vaccine that could be taken orally. A three-dose course of the Sabin vaccine provides a lifetime immunity against polio.

Another Polio Vaccine

Jonas Salk's vaccine brought polio under control in the United States. However, there were some concerns about its long-term effectiveness. Because the vaccine was made from dead viruses, experts were unsure how long it would continue to produce antibodies.

For this reason, Polish American researcher Albert Sabin began to look for strains of the polio virus that were too weak to produce the disease but strong enough to produce antibodies and keep producing them as long as the virus remained in the body. The vaccine he developed had the added advantage that it could be taken orally instead of being injected.

Sabin tested his vaccine on himself and then on prisoner volunteers. In 1957, his vaccine was used in the Soviet Union and eastern Europe. Three years later, it came into widespread use in the United States.

Today, American infants are routinely given Sabin polio vaccine. In this country, and anywhere else that polio vaccines have been used consistently, polio has virtually disappeared.

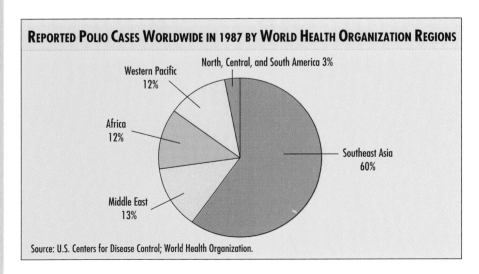

REPORTED POLIO CASES WORLDWIDE IN 1987 BY WORLD HEALTH ORGANIZATION REGIONS

North, Central, and South America 3%
Western Pacific 12%
Africa 12%
Middle East 13%
Southeast Asia 60%

Source: U.S. Centers for Disease Control; World Health Organization.

Plate Tectonics

The discovery that the earth's crust consists of moving plates helped to explain volcanoes, earthquakes, and new mountains.

Pieces of a Puzzle

Have you ever heard the expression "as solid as the Rock of Gibraltar"? Just how solid is the Rock of Gibraltar, or any other rock on the earth? Most of the time, the rocks and soil beneath our feet seem very solid. At other times, the ground quakes or a volcano erupts, and nothing seems stable at all. For thousands of years, people wondered at these catastrophic events. Slowly, the explanation emerged.

This discovery started in the 16th century. Very soon after Europeans sailed to the Americas, mapmakers began charting the new territory. Before long, some scholars noticed that the east coast of South America and the west coast of Africa would fit together neatly—if they were not so far apart. Some even suggested the possibility that all the continents had once been joined together and then had been violently torn apart.

This idea received further support in the 19th century. Scientists discovered geologic formations and life forms on both sides of the Atlantic Ocean that seemed closely related. If Africa and South America had been connected in some ancient time, these similar life forms might have descended from a common ancestor.

The Continental Drift By the early 1900s, at least one scientist was ready to propose an explanation. Around 1912, German geologist Alfred Wegener proposed the theory of continental drift. He said that all the continents originally had been one landmass, which he called Pangaea. Over millions of years, Pangaea had broken up into several pieces that had drifted apart. He disagreed with the earlier suggestions that the separation had been violent in nature.

To many scientists, the idea of continents moving across the ocean floor made little sense. They continued to look for other ways to explain the similar life forms on both sides of the Atlantic. By the time of Wegener's death in 1930, very few geologists had accepted his theory.

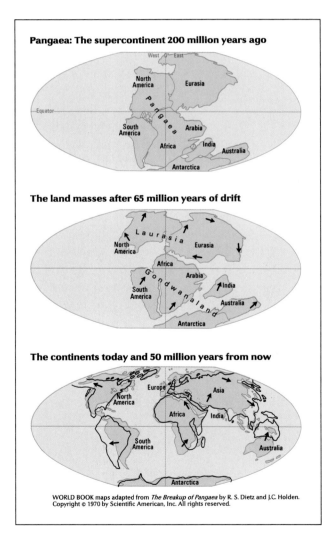

Pangaea: The supercontinent 200 million years ago

The land masses after 65 million years of drift

The continents today and 50 million years from now

The earth's surface consists of large rigid plates that are in continual motion and thus cause the continents to drift. These maps show past and future movement of the plates.

Plates in Motion

In the mid-1950s, two discoveries gave support to the idea that the continents were constantly in motion.

- Geologists had known that rocks are magnetized in a direction governed by the latitude of the place where they form. They discovered that on several continents rocks known to have been formed at earlier times had a different magnetic orientation from newer rocks found at the same location. This difference would suggest that the older rocks had been formed at a different latitude. The differences in magnetic orientation were not surprising if the continents were moving the way Wegener had proposed.

- Scientists studying the ocean floor discovered a mid-ocean ridge, or mountain range, that circled the globe from north to south and a canyon that ran the length of the ridge. They called the ridge and canyon the Great Global Rift.

These discoveries pointed to a possible mechanism for the movement of continents.

How It Works In 1960, geologist Harry Hess of Princeton University suggested that at the top of the mid-ocean ridge the ocean floor spreads apart as hot lava from beneath the earth's crust pushes up and forms new ocean floor. He also suggested that the earth's crust could slide and one piece could overlap another.

Scientists continued their investigations. Then in 1965, they proposed that the earth's surface consists of six large plates and several smaller ones. Since the plates are normally joined, they were named *tectonic plates,* from the Greek word for "carpenter."

Mid-ocean ridges are the boundaries that separate the plates. When plates bump into one another, they form new mountains and valleys.

When two plates slide past each other and overlap, a fault is created, and earthquakes frequently occur in that region.

This system and its motion is called plate tectonics. It differs from Wegener's theory of continental drift in the following way. Continental drift sees the continents as ships plowing through the ocean. Plate tectonics sees continents as rafts carried along with the flow.

THE RICHTER SCALE

In 1935, American seismologist Charles Richter developed a scale to measure the magnitude of earthquakes. Called the Richter Scale, it actually measures the sound waves emitted by the quake. The highest magnitude recorded in recent decades was the Alaska earthquake in 1964, which measured 8.3. Other recent quakes are listed here.

1985	Mexico City	8.1
1989	San Francisco	7.1
1994	Los Angeles	6.6

Earthquakes and volcanic eruptions occur along the boundaries of the tectonic plates. This photo shows recent earthquake damage in Los Angeles, California.

The New Geology

Plate tectonics changed geology by providing a theory to explain the behavior of the earth. At the same time, it explained phenomena that previously had been mysteries.

- Earthquakes: Plate tectonics suggests that earthquakes occur along faults, where one plate slides under the edge of another and creates an instability in the earth's crust. Current research may eventually enable scientists to predict the exact time and location of major quakes.

- Volcanoes: Most volcanoes occur at boundaries between plates. Volcanoes that do not occur along plate boundaries, like the Hawaiian island volcanoes, trace the past movements of a plate.

- Older Mountains: Studies suggest that the plates did not break apart only once but that they have been separating and joining repeatedly throughout time. Older mountains, such as the Laurentians in Canada and the Urals in the former Soviet Union—now in the middle of continents—may show where plates came together in the past.

Glossary

anesthetic: A drug that produces a loss of sensation, in one area (local) or throughout the body (general).

antibody: An agent in the body that fights disease by attacking foreign substances, such as viruses and bacteria, that enter the bloodstream.

antiseptic: A chemical that slows or stops the growth of harmful microorganisms to prevent infection.

atomic number: The number given to an element based on the number of protons, or positive charges, in its nucleus.

atomic weight: The weight of one single atom of an element.

beriberi: A disease caused by the lack of thiamine (Vitamin B_1) in a person's diet. The symptoms of beriberi include general weakness, swelling of body organs, and nerve damage.

big bang theory: A theory proposing that the universe was created by a giant explosion billions of years ago.

black body: A body or surface that absorbs all radiant energy and gives off no reflection.

black hole: A body in space that is thought to contain the remains of a star that collapsed. A black hole is thought to have immense gravitational pull.

botany: The branch of biology that deals with the study of plant life.

calculus: The branch of mathematics that deals with the study of continuously changing quantities, essential for studying bodies in motion.

carbohydrates: Nutrients rich in energy, found in sugars and starches, that are needed by the body in order for it to work properly.

cathode ray: Streams of electrons, or negatively charged particles, that are produced by electricity being forced through a glass vacuum tube.

chromosome: One of several rodlike structures in each cell that enables a cell to reproduce itself. Chromosomes contain genes, which carry a person's hereditary makeup.

circulatory system: The heart and network of arteries, veins, and capillaries that carry blood throughout the body.

conductor: A substance or body that allows heat, sound, or electricity to pass through it.

continental drift: The theory that all the continents were originally one huge landmass. Over millions of years, this mass broke into several smaller masses that drifted across the ocean floor. The original landmass was called Pangaea by Alfred Wegener, who proposed the theory.

convex lens: A lens that is curved or rounded like the outside of a sphere.

cross-pollination: The placement of pollen from one plant into the pistil (seed-producing part) of another plant. The plant produces a seed with two parents. The seed produces a new plant with the characteristics of both parent plants.

diabetes: A disease that prevents the body from properly processing sugar and other carbohydrates.

DNA: Deoxyribonucleic acid; an important nucleic acid found in all cells that carries the "blueprint" for inherited characteristics.

dominant: Having control over. In genetics, a dominant factor is a trait that will appear in offspring.

double helix: The double spiral, chainlike structure of a strand of DNA. Each side of the spiral contains nucleotides weakly linked to the other side, which can join or pull apart.

electron: One of the negatively charged particles that surround the nucleus of an atom.

electron microscope: A microscope in which a beam of electrons is used to enlarge the image of an object, similar to the way light is used to form an image in an ordinary microscope.

element: A substance that consists of atoms of only one kind, which cannot be broken down into a simpler substance.

elliptical: Oval-shaped.

fault: A break in the earth's crust that displaces rocks and causes the ground to become unstable.

fluorescence: A glow; the emission of light by an object when it is exposed to a certain kind of radiation, such as X rays or ultraviolet rays.

fossil fuel: A fuel, such as coal or oil, that is formed in the earth from the remains of dead plants and animals.

gene: Part of a DNA strand containing chemical information that influences inheritance. Genes are located in the chromosomes of a cell.

genetic engineering: A field of science that enables genes to be created, changed, or moved around by cutting DNA strands.

geology: The study of the history of the earth and its life, especially through the examination of rocks.

heredity: The transmission of physical and mental characteristics from parents to offspring through their genes.

insulin shock: The body's negative reaction to too much insulin and too little sugar in the blood.

Leyden jar: A metal-coated glass jar used for gathering and storing electricity. The metal coating helps to conduct the electricity.

mass: In physics, the amount of matter in a body.

microorganism: An organism, such as a virus or a bacterium, that is too small to be seen without the aid of a microscope.

natural selection: The tendency of nature to favor the inheritance of characteristics that promote a species' survival; the mechanism by which evolution works.

nitrous oxide: A colorless gas that is sometimes called laughing gas. When inhaled, it causes a loss of the ability to feel pain and sometimes produces laughter. It is used most commonly today by dentists.

nucleic acid: A complex molecule made of linked nucleotides that is found in all living cells. RNA and DNA are two important nucleic acids.

nucleotide: The basic unit of nucleic acid. A nucleotide is a chemical compound that combines with phosphoric acid to create nucleic acids.

penicillium: A type of mold from which the antibiotic penicillin is produced.

periodic law: The order that governs the composition of the elements, showing that elements with similar valences show a regular, or periodic, repetition of properties. Mendeleyev used this principle to arrange the elements on his periodic table.

photoelectric effect: The effect that causes an object struck by a bright light to give off electrons.

physics: The branch of science that deals with matter and energy and how they act upon each other. Physics includes the study of mechanics, heat, light, electricity, and atomic energy.

radiation: The emission of radiant energy in the form of electromagnetic waves or particles.

recessive: Not dominant. In genetics, a recessive factor will not appear in offspring if paired with a dominant factor, though it may be passed on to future offspring.

reflecting telescope: A telescope in which the main light-gathering element is a mirror.

refracting telescope: A telescope in which the main light-gathering element is a lens.

rickets: A disease of children that causes bones to become soft and misshapen. The lack of Vitamin D in the diet makes the body unable to absorb calcium and phosphorus, two minerals important for healthy bones.

RNA: Ribonucleic acid; one of several nucleic acids found in cells that help control cell activities.

scurvy: A disease caused by the lack of Vitamin C. Symptoms of scurvy include weakness, bleeding gums, and muscle soreness.

self-pollination: The placement of pollen from a plant into the pistil (seed-producing part) of the same plant.

sphygmomanometer: An instrument for measuring blood pressure, especially arterial blood.

subatomic particle: A particle smaller than an atom; a particle inside an atom.

tectonic plate: One of the six large and several smaller plates that make up the earth's crust. The plates may move and react with one another to cause earthquakes and, over a long period of time, create mountains and valleys.

vaccine: A preparation containing weakened or killed viruses or bacteria, which is administered to give a person active immunity to a certain disease.

valence: The combining power of an atom—that is, the number of times the electrons of an atom can form a chemical link with the electrons of another atom.

wavelength: The distance between any point in a light or sound wave to the same point in the next wave of the series.

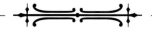

Suggested Readings

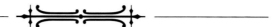

Note: An asterisk (*) denotes a Young Adult title.

Asimov, Isaac. *Asimov's Chronology of Science and Discovery*. Harper & Row, 1989.

———. *Atom: Journey Across the Subatomic Cosmos*. Dutton, 1991.

*Avraham, Regina. *The Circulatory System*. Chelsea House, 1989.

*Beyer, Don E. *The Manhattan Project: America Makes the First Atomic Bomb*. Franklin Watts, 1991.

*Biel, Timothy L. *Atoms: Building Blocks of Matter*. Lucent Books, 1990.

*Bridgman, Roger. *Electronics*. Dorling Kindersley, 1993.

*Brown, Fern G. *Hereditary Diseases*. Franklin Watts, 1987.

*Eagles, Douglas. *Nutritional Diseases*. Franklin Watts, 1987.

*Fachlam, Margery and Howard. *Healing Drugs: The History of Pharmacology*. Facts on File, 1992.

*Fradin, Dennis B. *Medicine: Yesterday, Today, and Tomorrow*. Children's Press, 1989.

Franch, Irene M., and Brownstone, David M. *Scientists and Technologists*. "Work Throughout History" series. Facts on File, 1988.

*Gallant, Roy A. *Before the Sun Dies: The Story of Evolution*. Macmillan, 1989.

*Grady, Sean M. *Marie Curie*. Lucent Books, 1992.

*———. *Plate Tectonics—Earth's Shifting Crust*. Lucent Books, 1991.

*Hann, Judith. *How Science Works*. Reader's Digest, 1991.

*Hitzeroth, Deborah. *Telescopes: Searching the Heavens*. Lucent Books, 1991.

*Hooper, Tony. *Genetics*. "Breakthrough" series. Raintree Steck-Vaughn, 1994.

*McGowan, Tom. *Chemistry: The Birth of a Science*. Franklin Watts, 1989.

*———. *The Circulatory System: From Harvey to the Artificial Heart*. Franklin Watts, 1988.

*McTavish, Douglas. *Isaac Newton*. Franklin Watts, 1990.

*Nardo, Don. *Germs: Mysterious Microorganisms*. Lucent Books, 1991.

Newhouse, Elizabeth L. *Inventors and Discoverers: Changing Our World*. National Geographic Society, 1988.

*Parker, Steve. *Charles Darwin and Evolution*. HarperCollins, 1992.

*Sherrow, Victoria. *Great Scientists*. Facts on File, 1992.

*Stewart, Gail B. *Microscopes: Bringing the Unseen World Into Focus*. Lucent Books, 1992.

*Swisher, Clarice. *Relativity: Opposing Viewpoints*. Greenhaven Press, 1990.

*Tames, Richard. *Louis Pasteur*. Franklin Watts, 1990.

*Tauber, Gerald E. *Relativity: From Einstein to Black Holes*. Franklin Watts, 1988.

*Van Rose, Susanna. *Volcano and Earthquake*. Knopf, 1992.

*Veglahn, Nancy. *Women Scientists*. Facts on File, 1991.

Wilson, Trevor I. *Science: A History of Discovery in the 20th Century*. Oxford, 1990.

Index

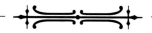